Praise for *Work with Passion*

"Nancy Anderson shows you how you can create your ideal job....
Thorough, inspiring, and richly documented, *Work with Passion* shows
that the process of seeking what one loves and turning it into a successful career is not only possible but logical."

— *San Diego Tribune*

"[Anderson] sets out to help readers identify their passions and determine how those interests can translate into a career that pays the bills.
More emotionally charged than most career books, this volume also
delves into the meaning of personal history and childhood events, and
carefully considers feelings, self-perception and motivation. Points
are illustrated with detailed real-life stories of Anderson's clients....
Anderson's thorough process goes beyond simply identifying what
one wants to do and explains how to research, network and even strike
out on one's own in order to achieve a passion-worthy career."

— *Publishers Weekly*

"Anderson weaves a brilliant path for those who are seeking aspects for
a greater life, which may have been elusive up till now.... She un-
leashes the perfect formula for the rational and creative selves within
us to recognize and therefore pursue their own unique way for finding
their purpose and creating a passionate life. *Work with Passion* is a great
gift to others and for self."

— *New Connexion: Pacific Northwest's Journal of Conscious Living*

"A wonderful book ... packed with inspiring advice."

— *New Age Retailer*

"An effective road map for discovering a truly rewarding career."

— *NAPRA Review*

"Gives solid advice."

— *The Bookwatch*

WORK WITH
PASSION
IN MIDLIFE
AND BEYOND

WORK WITH
PASSION
IN MIDLIFE
AND BEYOND

Reach Your
Full Potential
& Make the
Money You Need

Nancy Anderson

New World Library
Novato, California

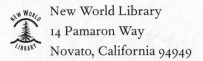 New World Library
14 Pamaron Way
Novato, California 94949

Text design by Tona Pearce Myers

Library of Congress Cataloging-in-Publication Data
Anderson, Nancy.
 Work with passion in midlife and beyond : reach your full potential & make the money you need / Nancy Anderson.
     p.   cm.
Includes bibliographical references and index.
ISBN 978-1-57731-694-7 (pbk. : alk. paper)
 1. Job satisfaction. 2. Middle-aged persons—Employment. 3. Success in business. I. Title.
 HF5549.5.J63.A533 2010
 650.1084'4—dc22   2009051333

First printing, March 2010
ISBN 978-1-57731-694-7
Printed in Canada on 100% postconsumer-waste recycled paper

g New World Library is a proud member of the Green Press Initiative.

10 9 8 7 6 5 4 3 2 1

You experience life when you feel yourself
to be free and useful and joyous,
unconscious of either fear or doubt.
— EMMET FOX

Contents

Introduction

Midlife and beyond is when the authentic self emerges through layers of family and cultural conditioning to find answers to questions of ultimate concern: who am I, why am I here, and what should I do with the rest of my life? This creative core of your personality wants emotional and spiritual fulfillment, not only for you but also for society at large. By contrast, in your twenties and thirties you wanted to go for the personal gold, attract sexual and marriage partners, have and bring up children, experiment with many career and lifestyle options, try on different personas, and compete with peers for status and recognition.

Navigating the transition into the second stage of life takes courage and persistence, since your younger self holds on with all its might in a culture that values outer success more than inner success. Continuing to pursue sexual and material goals provokes the well-known midlife crisis, with its regressive symptoms of alienation and depression. The solution is to let go of values that have outlived their usefulness so that life energy can be redirected into goals appropriate at this stage of life, particularly in your work.

Given the volatile economy, rising costs of living, and likelihood that safety nets like social security, dividends from investments, and savings may not cover expenses when you are older, it is imperative that you start *now* to find the work that engages your heart and soul. It is not just a matter of *if* you should follow your passion. You absolutely must find the work that gives your life meaning in order to weather the turmoil that will be around for some time to come. The stakes simply could not be higher.

Discovering what you do naturally and well after a lifetime of experience is not easy, since you probably take your strengths for granted. You don't even think about what you're doing; you just do it. It doesn't occur to you that you can get paid to solve the problems that fascinate you (passion clue), at your own pace and in your own way. But when you do the work that comes naturally, you will get better and better at it as you age, and your expertise will make you virtually recession-proof. And once you are in the niche that nourishes your soul and serves others, you will be the center of calm in a stormy world.

To use a business analogy, to survive and thrive in difficult times, owners and managers have to focus on what they do best. They don't allow fear to distract them from taking the action they need to take. Inventory or services that are not selling are eliminated to make room for what will sell. Outdated software is replaced to improve communication at all levels. Change for the better can be disruptive and uncomfortable, but streamlining the operation sets the stage for new and more profitable ways to serve consumers.

Similarly, to survive and thrive in midlife and beyond, you need to start by facing your fears, which I show you how to do in the second chapter. You will also learn how to eliminate the distractions that keep you stuck in the past: clutter; possessions; illogical beliefs about yourself, money, and work; and self-destructive habits like spending time with people who drain your energy. With distractions out of the way (and it will take a while to eliminate them), the next step is to rewrite your life story, following the outline discussed in the third chapter. To create a happy ending to your story, you will need to look at the past with ruthless honesty, examining the types of choices you made that always ended in failure, some of which you may still make, as well as the types of choices that always turned out well. Choices that always worked for you hold the key to your passion, because that is when you trusted your instincts.

Since finding your niche in midlife and beyond is like solving a mystery, in the fourth chapter you will learn about the five passion clues that let you know you are on the right path and the five off-track signals that tell you when you are off, way off, the passion path. Some of these clues and signals you already know; others will surprise you.

In the fifth chapter you will create a template for success, beginning by defining your strengths, what you do easily after decades of practice. The next step is to identify your values, what is important to you now that you are older. Then you will make a list of your needs, what you must have to feel happy and productive. As a group, your strengths, values, and needs define the perfect niche and your place within that niche. This template for success also helps you to target the right customers, clients, or employers, since these people have the same values and they need your strengths in order to solve their problems. In mutually beneficial business relationships, everyone's needs are met.

The sixth chapter shows you how to make the small changes that get you in the habit of succeeding. Since the subconscious is slow to accept change, even change for the better, you will learn how to write goals using words the subconscious will accept as logical. Writing and rewriting until what you write makes sense allows your emotions to catch up with your intellect.

To visualize what your authentic self defines as success in midlife and beyond, you will make a collage of images and words you select from magazines or download from the Internet. The finished collage will surprise you, and at the same time it will feel strangely familiar. Later you will see that your ideal niche was right there in the collage.

Whether the niche where you will grow to your full potential is a full- or part-time job, a business, a solo practice, or a creative project that you work on by yourself: the seventh chapter provides guidelines for gathering information, holding low-pressure meetings with decision makers who share your passion, and negotiating salaries, fees, and offers. You will also discover your personality type — whether you are a partner type, team type, or solo type, an introvert or an extrovert — the size of organization best for you, and whether you are an entrepreneur.

The eighth and final chapter concludes with a description of the happy ending, otherwise known as unfamiliar territory. In this happy ending you are in your perfect niche: you work with people you like and admire and who like and admire you, doing what you love so much that you would do the work for nothing. You savor the rewards of success on your terms: peace, prosperity, and joy.

Throughout *Work with Passion in Midlife and Beyond*, I have included inspirational stories about people like you who are doing the work they enjoy and making the money they need, beginning and concluding with Ann's story to show the process she went through to become the authentic individual she is today. As I did with all the stories in the book, I changed her name and some of her circumstances to protect her privacy. You may not have all the challenges Ann had to face and overcome before she reached her destination, but her courage and determination will inspire you to do whatever it takes to create your happy ending.

At the end of the book, you will find a list of helpful resources: books, websites, and television shows that demonstrate the three stages of change that lead to success in any endeavor.

I suggest that you read all the way through the book before doing any of the exercises. By the time you finish the last chapter, you will know what needs your attention and where you are doing just fine, although you will still want to do all the exercises. You may want to work with a coach or a passion buddy who can encourage you when you experience the delays and setbacks that are a normal part of the creative process.

The Aha! moment can occur anytime, but the chapters in the book are designed to be read in the order in which they appear — so don't skip exercises because you think that will speed up the process. Instead, stay focused on the chapter you are in, not on the outcome. Taking time to hold still and reflect will consolidate gains and lock in learning. Traveling at a slow, steady pace will also allow you to enjoy the journey to finding passion in midlife and beyond.

CHAPTER 1

Ann Rewrites Her Life Story

To a mind that is still, the whole universe surrenders.
— CHUANG-TZU

Ann was like most of the seventy-eight million people who are in or beyond midlife: she wanted to use her talent and experience in work that would give her life meaning and purpose (passion clue!) and to make all the money she needed. Her goal was to wake up every morning looking forward to a new day of challenge and growth. But she wasn't sure how to make that dream a reality — she didn't know the specific steps to take and in what order to take them.

Ann's life was an overgrown jungle when she came to me for help with her career and life goals. She was fifty years old and in a troubled second marriage. She and her husband had two spoiled teenagers who pitted the parents against each other. Her environment reflected her mental confusion — even her garage and storage spaces looked like dumping grounds. Ann's inept boss, the son of the owner of the company, expected her to treat him like a crown prince to whom she owed her livelihood. Whenever she suggested ways to improve their operations, he dismissed her ideas as unrealistic.

"I can't figure out why my life is such a struggle," Ann told me when we met in my home office. "All I want is to be happy." She had emailed the first part of her autobiography to me before we met (writing an autobiography of approximately fifty pages is my clients' first assignment, although some clients write longer stories; the length of the project is up to them). After reading Ann's story I wasn't surprised to hear that she was struggling.

"That may be what you want consciously, Ann," I said. "But subconsciously your story is right on track."

"What do you mean?" Ann asked, looking startled.

"I mean that you're following a life script you set in motion around the age of puberty, one based on illogical conclusions you made while growing up in your family," I replied, motioning to the folder on my coffee table that contained the pages of her story. "Disappointment is the outcome you expect. So you keep making choices that guarantee that ending. If you want to change the story, you'll have to write a new ending, with you as the Victor not the Victim."

Thinking of herself as a character in a story whose ending she decided a long time ago gave Ann a new way to look at the past and at her present predicament. It hadn't occurred to her that the irrational decisions she made when she was too young to know what she was doing were the source of her failures at home and work. Ann also was not aware that her life script included men who let her make their decisions and then accused her of being too controlling.

"Why do I keep marrying the same kind of man?" Ann asked wearily. "I thought my husband was different when I met him. He was fun to be with, and he said he liked being with me. But after we were married, he started finding fault and withholding affection and praise. When I set limits with our teenagers, he says I'm too harsh. No matter what happens, it's my fault. I feel like it's them against me."

What Ann was experiencing was predictable, given her assumption that she was responsible for everything. I told her that if she wanted the situation to improve, she'd have to stop what she was doing that wasn't working. As a first step, I suggested she take alcohol out of her system. "A couple of glasses of wine a day can be therapeutic for some people," I said. "But you're using alcohol to numb your feelings. And you need to know what you feel so you can make better choices."

I also asked Ann to start her day with ten minutes of prayer and meditation and to repeat this routine before she went to sleep at night. "Pausing to reflect will help you break the habit of acting without thinking," I said. "As it is, you're on automatic pilot, repeating a story that always ends in failure."

Setting aside time to reflect was not Ann's modus operandi. Her way of solving problems was to jump in and think later; otherwise she felt guilty about not doing enough. When she was still for too long, she started feeling anxious. To distract herself she took on more responsibility. Ann's autobiography revealed that her habit of overextending herself was the way she distracted herself from the chaos in her family, where drinking, fighting, and inertia were the norm. She had not experienced respectful boundaries and conflict resolution, the characteristics of a functional family.

"I see why stagnation is the outcome I expect," Ann said, after we talked at length about the life script concept. "Nothing ever got better in my family. Even now, everything is just as it was in the past. It's the same with me. No matter what I do, nothing gets better. I feel as though I'm waking up from a bad dream. It's embarrassing to think of what I've done to myself and my children."

Remorse is the first feeling that surfaces when my clients become aware of what they have done to themselves and allowed others to do to them. Although awakening from the spell of the script can be a jolt, this shock is the precursor to positive change.

"Well, you can't blame yourself for what you did when you weren't conscious. What's important is what you do now that you're awake," I said to Ann. "The next time your husband asks you what to do, don't give him the answer. Let him think it through or not think it through."

"But what if he accuses me of not caring about him?"

"Ah, so you're afraid he'll think you are an uncaring person if you let him struggle. But isn't it caring to say you know that if he thinks about the problem long enough, he'll come up with a better solution than anything you could imagine?" When Ann looked doubtful, I laughed and said, "You see? You believe he can't figure out his problems. So no wonder you charge in with answers. That's what I meant by stopping what you're doing that isn't working. But don't expect change to be easy. The script won't go away without a fight."

Dismantling a life script is similar to a home remodel that starts with taking down the existing framing. In Ann's case the "framing" was her assumption that people couldn't figure out their problems, a conclusion she made while growing up with people who did not solve their problems. So Ann got involved with other people who didn't solve their problems, because these people were familiar.

Ann and the people close to her were caught in what psychiatrist Stephen Karpman calls the Drama Triangle. They switched back and forth among all three of the roles in the triangle: Victim, Rescuer, and Persecutor, sometimes in the same conversation.

The Drama Triangle is so pervasive that if you listen carefully, you will hear it wherever you go. A conversation may go from "poor me" (Victim) to "let me help you" (Rescuer) to "it's all your/their fault" (Persecutor). The end result of these interactions is always failure, since the goal of a life script is to prove that life is an exercise in futility.[1]

"Start with small steps. This will lead to greater changes," I said to Ann. I asked her not to quit her job in a huff, for example, which is what Ann would have done in the past (as if to say, "I'll show you"), but rather to change her sales strategy. "Your boss's indiscriminate approach to sales is out of date," I said. "Today you have to be selective and build trust with customers, and that takes patience and a genuine desire to serve them. Stop calling on people who take up your time with no return. Instead, target customers who need what you have to offer."

Since Ann's overly conscientious nature also encouraged her teenagers to turn over to her too much responsibility for their lives, I suggested that she moderate her efforts on their behalf. "Your kids are almost adults now, long past the age when they need to be told what to do," I said. "When they 'forget' to do their homework or they're late for school, let them experience the consequences. Set clear guidelines and stick to them, including quiet time for them to recharge their batteries."

And I suggested that when Ann's husband blamed her for anything, she not retaliate. "Listen to what he says without interrupting. If he's right, apologize and correct the problem. If he's wrong, say you disagree and leave it at that. He has a life script too. If you stop trying to change him, that won't fit his script — what he expects of women. Don't look to him for validation. Just notice your reaction when he disagrees with you."

"That's it? I don't understand how that will change things," Ann said, looking puzzled.

"Awareness changes everything, Ann," I said, smiling. "Give it a try. In time you'll see what I mean. If you need to talk about it, call me."

To create a happy ending to their life stories, my clients have to do what feels unfamiliar and uncomfortable, such as trusting their intuition. This is difficult to do when the people close to them are not going through the same process. But if they persist, they learn to live without the need for agreement.

"I know that some people, including some therapists, say partners are supposed to validate each other, that it's a sign of love and support. But that only leads to more enmeshment, not a sense of separate identity," I said to Ann when she looked skeptical. "It's just like in your family: there are no boundaries — everybody's stuck together like a box of melted chocolates. I assure you that once you change for the better, others will adapt or leave your life."

When Ann seemed uneasy, I asked if anything else was bothering her. After taking a deep breath, she confessed she had been meeting a man for lunch. "Nothing's happened," she hastily assured me. "We just meet for lunch. I really look forward to seeing him. He's always telling me how wonderful I am, and this makes me feel appreciated."

"Thank you for telling me, Ann," I said. "If you'd held back this information, the process would have bogged down and I wouldn't have known why. My question is, how do you feel about a man who knowingly spends time with a married woman?"

After she thought for a moment, Ann replied, "I wouldn't trust him."

"And isn't that the script, to fall for untrustworthy men and then get disappointed when they let you down?"

Ann's eyes opened wide. "I never thought of it that way."

The key phrase here is "I never thought..." Agreeing to meet an untrustworthy man for lunch only reinforced Ann's "men always let me down" script, which put her in the Victim role.

"I realize your emotional needs are not being met by your husband," I said. "But affairs aren't the solution. In fact, they're a distraction. End the lunches; then you'll feel better about yourself."

Since clutter was another distraction that let Ann avoid uncomfortable feelings, I asked her to get rid of everything except what she loved and used. "When you feel anxious about getting rid of some of the stuff, ask what part of the past those items represent. Then think about what life will be like when you wake up and all you see is what you love and use."

I also suggested that Ann cut back on spending. "You and your husband need to sit down and agree on how much money you can save. When you have a cushion, you won't have to make career decisions based on the need for money."

Ann took copious notes while I was talking, as she did in subsequent sessions, dedication that is typical of clients who complete the passion process. By the time they leave their sessions with me, they're already putting the changes I suggested in motion. As Ann gathered up her belongings, she said she never would have made the connection between her failures and fear of the unknown. "But that makes sense. I knew I was doing something wrong, but I didn't know where to begin," Ann said, pausing at the door to my home office. "Now that I'm aware of the script, I can and will change it. I'm not sure who I am, much less what I need. But at this point I'm so desperate I'll do whatever it takes to change."

"That's exactly when we change, Ann — when we're desperate," I said, and we both laughed.

Ann went to work changing her script over the next few weeks. First, she called the man she had been seeing to say there would be no more lunches. Then she set up a schedule to organize her surroundings, since she knew that without a deadline, the project would become another distraction. She went through every drawer, closet, and room in her home, discarding items that had outlived their usefulness.

"Just asking 'Do I love this?' really helps," Ann said when she called to update me on her progress. "Hardly anything meets that criterion. I was really out of touch with myself. I still don't know who I am or what I need, but I'm getting better."

"Better is a realistic goal," I said, and we laughed, since Ann had a habit of setting her goals too high and then feeling discouraged when she failed (this was part of her script).

At first Ann's husband balked when she asked for assistance in the purging process, but when he realized Ann was serious he got on board. Her kids got excited about the project after Ann told them they could split the profits from whatever they sold on eBay. The entire family held a garage sale to get rid of bigger items; the stuff that was left over they donated to charities or took to the dump. Afterward, they celebrated with a dinner at the family's favorite pizza restaurant.

Simultaneously, Ann stopped calling on nonproductive customers and started a campaign to get new ones. Within three months she landed two large accounts, which surprised her boss. By the end of the year, Ann was known as the sales champ in the company. Then the owner started using her as an example of how to sell.

It was harder for Ann to stop telling her husband what to do; old habits die a slow death. But she did better with her teenagers. When they complained, acted helpless, or gave Ann the silent treatment, she spoke from her heart, not her head. "I hope you'll forgive me for teaching you to expect me to do everything for you," Ann said to her teenagers. "That made you dependent on me, so no wonder you're angry with me. I want you to believe that you can solve your problems, and the only way that's going to happen is for you to make choices and learn from them. You're both smart people, and you know what you need to do. I'm here, and so is your father. If you need help or you want to talk, all you have to do is ask."

Easier said than done. But Ann was determined to change, so she corrected herself when she relapsed into old ways, and she tried not to beat herself up when change took longer than she expected. As the months went by, she saw the benefit of letting people learn from their own choices, or not learn from them.

Ann's biggest test came the following Christmas when the family went to her family's home to celebrate the holidays. She had been dreading the visit because she was afraid guilt would push her back into the Rescuer role. But Ann was pleasantly surprised by what happened. "Christmas actually went very well," Ann wrote in a cheery email to me. "I made a decision not to drink this year. I had a glass of wine with Christmas dinner, and that was it. It's still difficult for me to be around people 24/7 for three days straight, but it's much more manageable when I'm not drinking."

Ann called a few weeks later to say she was depressed by the Christmas visit. I told her that given her decision to spend three days and nights under the same roof with people who refused to face their problems, it wasn't surprising that depression was the outcome.

"But I thought I handled the visit so well," Ann exclaimed. "I came away feeling much better this time."

"You did do better, Ann, but where you went wrong is that you hoped others would be better and they weren't," I said. "Once you admitted this, you felt depressed. I think you were feeling happy before the visit because of the improvements you've made, and you felt guilty about that. To right the imbalance, you agreed to go for the visit, and then your spirits sank because nothing had changed. Now you're back in familiar territory, feeling hopeless and depressed."

The purpose I serve for my clients is to put into words what they can't or won't admit. They become more comfortable with honesty as they go through the process of finding their passion. Once they see others as they are, not as they want them to be, including family members, my remodeling work is done, although some clients continue to work with me to maintain clarity and focus.

"You're right, I was feeling guilty about being happy," Ann said the next time we met. "It took me a while to understand what you meant, that it felt uncomfortable to be happy, and so I made poor choices to feel comfortable again. I was even starting to have hope for a better future."

"Guilt is a formidable adversary, Ann. It can make us do what we don't want to do, including what's harmful to us," I said. "But guilt withers away in the face of honest feelings. The next time you visit your family, limit your stay to a few hours. If you remain overnight, rent rooms in a hotel. Keep the boundaries firm. Then you won't feel depressed."

Ann said she also felt depressed when her husband criticized her in front of her family. "He's done that before and I ignored it," Ann said. "But this time I listened to my feelings. And I was *angry*. But rather than snap back or seethe in silence, as I would have done before, I asked if he'd step into the other room. After we sat down, I asked him to stop putting me down and told him that if he did it again I would leave."

"He must have been surprised by how calm you were," I said.

"He was. He said he was only kidding. I said, 'No, you weren't kidding, you wanted to hurt me, and I want you to stop. If you are angry with me, let me know what's bothering you so I can address it, but don't use sarcasm and put-downs.' He said he was sorry and that he wouldn't do it again."

Ann knew better than to expect instant results, but she said that since she and her husband had gotten back home, he'd been more thoughtful. "He knows I want him to change for himself, not for me. I let him know that it's up to him to see the value in being respectful. Letting him make that decision has changed the dynamic in our marriage."

Now that she was able to set good boundaries without feeling wrong or guilty, Ann was ready to find the work that made her feel free, useful, and creative. So she started the process of meeting with people to find her niche, using the techniques covered in chapter 7. In a few months Ann received offers from several prospective employers. "After meeting with dozens of people in my areas of interest," she told me, "I decided that I need to have my own business. I could take another sales job and make money, but there's no challenge in that. My husband and I have saved every extra penny so that I could do what I want to do. I really connected with people who owned their own small recruiting businesses. They told me I was a natural for this work; one said she would love to have me join her, so I'm taking her up on the offer."

Working with an experienced entrepreneur would provide Ann with invaluable instruction. And she wouldn't have to worry about carrying the overhead while she was learning. Ann agreed with me when I told her this, adding, "Rookie mistakes can put you out of business. But I'm at the stage of life where I have to do things my way, so after I've learned the basics I'll go on my own, and my new partner is fine with that. Just the thought of being in my own business scares me to death, so I know that must be my passion."

Their passion is often what scares my clients, because they think they can't survive doing what they love. They're afraid they will wind up pushing a grocery cart down a lonely street. The temptation is to stay with what they know and then die a slow death. But if they take the small steps that lead to their passion, as Ann did, they can't fail; they can only grow.

Ann is sixty years old now and enjoying life to the fullest as an independent recruiter, specializing in finding salespeople and sales managers for her business clients. There were trials and setbacks along the way. Some days she felt like giving up, but she didn't. "Persistence is my middle name now," Ann told me, laughing, when we met again. "I never would have made it without your encouragement. Other self-employed people helped too, particularly women. Like you, they told me to listen to myself and to not get distracted by others' negativity. Thankfully, I've learned to tune out the negative people. I feel blessed; all my prayers have been answered."

Ann's clients see her as the answer to their prayers, as does her husband, who is her biggest fan. "He went through his own transformation after he met with you several times. He really appreciated both your direct approach and what he learned from writing his autobiography. He realized he was repeating his father's passive-aggressive script," Ann said to me in a recent conversation. "Now that our values are in sync, we get along well."

When I asked about her business, Ann said she doubted she would ever retire. "I may cut back as I age, but I'd miss my clients and candidates if I stopped working altogether. They talk to me about everything — kids, family, romances, you name it. It's a wonderfully freeing way to work. Essentially, I get paid to be me."

Ann said she had also started writing a blog on sales for a website. "The editor and I have much in common," Ann said. "She struggles with maintaining boundaries too. I like writing about what I've learned from my years in sales — what works, what doesn't work. My readers are younger than I am, web-savvy folks like my candidates. My age doesn't matter to them; what matters is that what I know helps them to succeed."

I had noticed Ann's writing ability while reading her autobiography, so I wasn't surprised she was using that skill to pass on what she knew about sales. Using what they know to help others succeed is typical of my older clients once they get in the right niche, and this generosity comes back to them in full measure.

When I asked about Ann's son and daughter, she said they were doing well. "Our son decided to work his way around the world after high school, and we encouraged him to do just that; he'd lived such a sheltered life. A couple of years later he went to college and got a degree. Now he works for one of those social networking sites. He's married to a sweet young woman; we get along well.

"Our daughter is in South America with a nondenominational group that helps young women build self-confidence; she writes us newsy emails about her adventures. I'm pleased she uses her writing talent to promote a worthy cause. She's engaged to a man who respects her boundaries. She said she remembered that I told her to make mutual respect a priority," Ann said with a self-deprecating laugh. "She and her brother both say they're proud of what I've achieved and of the person I've become."

"It must have taken time for them to adjust to the new you, Ann," I said. "How did you know when they saw you as a person, not just as their mom?"

"It was when they thanked me for not making it easy for them when they hit a rough patch," Ann said. "They said they knew it was because I loved them and wanted them to be independent."

Ann said her biggest challenge was (and still is) to stay detached when the people she loves are struggling. "You want to save them from the pain, but that was my mistake earlier," she said. "That's what I saw my mother and grandmother do: they took care of everybody and crippled them in the process. Then they felt resentful about being burdened. No wonder they were never happy.

"My kids didn't always understand what I was doing," Ann said. "Certainly not my family; they were always quick to blame or criticize me for not doing enough, although that's changed now that both my parents have passed on. My son and daughter said the way I handled my family's disapproval showed them how to respond when others disapproved of them."

"That's the ultimate reward of being true to yourself, Ann, when your grown children copy that example," I said, smiling. The happy ending to her story was not what Ann had expected; it was much better. Rewriting the life script that caused the misery in her life was scary because she was certain disaster would strike if she turned her attention to what she wanted to do. To Ann's relief, letting go of the need to be in control was the best decision she ever made, not only for her but also for those she loved.

Redefining Work

Earlier in life Ann had heard the voice that urged her to find the work that made her heart sing. But because of family and financial obligations, she had stayed in jobs she disliked. Like many people, she thought it was not possible to make money doing what she enjoyed. Enjoyment was for after work, weekends, and vacations. Passion was for a lucky few. She felt fortunate just to have a job, especially in hard times.

The definition of work as survival runs deep in the individual and collective subconscious, with good reason. Current and past economic downturns, global competition, and the fear of poverty compel many people to stay with what they know rather than risk the unknown. But when you sacrifice fulfillment for money, you feel a deep sense of futility. If this is all there is to life, then what's the point of living?

The years in midlife and beyond offer an opportunity to find the niche where you will reach your full potential. Rather than work for money, you can work for love and make money. Instead of living according to others' definitions of success, you can redefine success so that it reflects what you value at this stage of life. But how do you know what you value? How can you discover who you are after a lifetime of being the person you thought you were supposed to be? How do you dig down through the layers of fear and conditioning to find your authentic self? What if (gulp) there is no one there?

In the following chapters, you'll discover how to find your self, define what you value, and use what you learned to find your niche. Your niche is the place where you can say what you think and feel without fear of criticism or retaliation, making your life about what you love, not what you "have" to do.

You'll experience setbacks and delays along the way, and this is to be expected, so don't feel discouraged by them. A setback or delay is not failure as much as a signal that you're going back to what's familiar, if only to find out you don't have to do that anymore. Repeating the past is seductive because it's what you know, and the future is scary because you haven't experienced it before. But being open to the new keeps you forever young and interesting.

Change takes determination and courage, so avoid people whose ambivalence and pessimism will drag you down. Instead, surround yourself with what will encourage you and uplift your spirits: art, music, dance, nature, and people whose hearts are on their sleeves, not in their bank accounts.

No book can replace professional guidance, although books can provide encouragement and information. So if you can afford it, hire a coach or a counselor to help you stay on track, someone who will hold you accountable. Or you can ask a trusted friend to be a passion buddy, and you can do the same for that person.

As you work through the steps in this book, on your own or with your coach or passion buddy, exercise regularly, eat and drink in moderation, and rest *before* you feel tired. A healthy mind, body, and spirit adapt more readily to change for the better.

As with all the other heroes and heroines in *Work with Passion in Midlife and Beyond*, when you know who you are and what you value, and you are true to those values, you will say, "Wow. Look at me. I created the life I was born to live."

SUMMARY

1. What are your current circumstances?
2. Are these circumstances the outcome you expected?
3. Do you want to change?
4. Will you ask for help when you need it?
5. Can you persevere when change takes longer than you expect?

CHAPTER 2

Streamline Your Life

Fear of the unknown is really fear of losing the known.
— KRISHNAMURTI

As with any process that leads to a happy ending, change for the better takes place in three stages. The first stage is when you admit that what you're doing is not working, and you ask for help if you need it. Then comes the second and most difficult stage, *stopping* what you're doing that is not working. If you persist in your efforts, you reach the third and final stage, making choices that work for you. You may relapse occasionally, but you rebound quickly.

To add to your confusion in the second stage of change, people who feel upset by the changes you are making will use tactics to undermine your resolve, such as trying to make you feel guilty or obligated to them. The anxiety can be so intense that you give in to the pressure and go back to what you know, even though it causes you pain. If you try again (and again!), healthy choices become familiar and comfortable.

Paradoxically, healthy choices feel wrong because they're the opposite of what you think you should do or were taught to do. Whenever you do what you are not "supposed" to do, up come your worst fears: What if I'm wrong? What if I hurt someone? What if I wind up alone and lonely? What if there's no such thing as a happy ending? To relieve the discomfort, you go back to what is familiar, as when you try to make someone happy and fail (failure is what you know).

If you stop trying to make people happy, that feels wrong because you think you are giving up on or abandoning them. You're afraid they will think you don't care about them, or that you are selfish if you focus on what you want to do. Yet detachment is the solution, because it puts responsibility for the other person's happiness where it belongs, on the other person.

Once you stop trying to make people happy, they will create new problems to get you back into the struggle for power. If you get taken in by this tactic, you'll revert to controlling behavior and you will be back in the past again, and now both of you will be unhappy. (You have heard that it takes two to tango?)

In a 2007 *U.S. News and World Report* article about why we continue to make poor choices, the author says the problem is based on how our brains are wired:

> Why do we make bad choices even when we know better? Part of [the reason] is that we are wired to care more about immediate, tangible consequences than about delayed and intangible consequences.... Is this hopeless then? How can people change their ways? The answer is to build systems into your life that reward healthy choices or that make healthy choices more convenient than unhealthy ones. People will naturally take the path of least resistance. Set up your lives or the lives of your children so that the path of least resistance is the path that you actually want to take.[1]

Ann (described in the previous chapter) kept trying to control her husband, a script she copied from her mother and grandmother, who had tried to control the men in their lives. But this only fosters resentment on the part of the men being controlled (who are likely to respond with "You can't tell *me* what to do").

At a deeper level, Ann's choice of husbands was a reflection of what she needed to change in herself. When the psyche wants to grow, it uses any means to call flaws to our attention, including partners who exhibit in living Technicolor what is true about us. By wrestling with her husband's lack of confidence, for example, Ann wrestled with her own fear of the unknown. In time, taking the risks that scared her became the path of least resistance, but not without a struggle. As happened to Ann, whenever you step into the unknown you feel confused and disoriented, like a tragic actor who is auditioning for the lead in a romantic comedy. If change is harder than you expect, you alter course, take shortcuts, or give up on the process.

When you reach the difficult stage of change, you need encouragement to persevere in your efforts, which is why I wrote this book. After all, how many people do you know who have reached their full potential and make the money they need?

When they were young, your grandparents and parents hoped to find steady jobs that paid the bills and provided for their children. If they were like most people, they could hardly wait to retire, if they lived that long. In addition, if your parents were young adults in the 1950s, their roles in life were clearly defined (although they may have changed those scripts in later decades). Mick LaSalle, a movie critic for the *San Francisco Chronicle*, summarizes marriage and work in the 1950s in his review of the movie *Revolutionary Road*: "For a man, it's a life sentence of unrewarding work. For a woman, it's a cell door closing. For both, it's a farewell to dreams."[2] Flash forward to today, and many people still believe you can't do what you love at *any* age and make a living. For them, work is a battle for money and status (that's why they call it work).

Fortunately, views of work are changing, thanks to your generation's good health and entrepreneurial spirit and the phenomenal growth in technology, the Internet, service and information businesses, and women's influence in the marketplace. Additionally, employers are also more open to hiring older, smart, productive people like you to solve their problems, particularly when judgment and the ability to get along with people are needed. Youth is a great commodity, but it is no match for the practical intelligence that comes after a lifetime of trial and error. The lessons learned from experience are even more valuable in volatile economic times, when waste is not an option.

In fact, some employers are concerned about what will happen if your generation retires en masse. They wonder who is going to fill the experience gap. Employers need not be concerned, since 83 percent of the people born between 1946 and 1964 say they plan to keep working after age sixty.[3] They want to extend their careers, change careers, or work flexible hours to accommodate their energetic lifestyles. According to *Business Week*, people who continue to work when they are older will add trillions to the gross national product. These folks may even eliminate the predicted shortfall in Social Security benefits if the mandatory retirement age rises to accommodate their desire to keep working. Thanks to you and your peers, the belief that creativity ends at fifty-five, sixty, or any age is dead and gone.[4]

The trend toward working past retirement age is only going to expand as the older-population curve moves further into the twenty-first century. Your expertise and maturity will be highly valued by employers, customers, and clients in the years to come, particularly in service and information businesses. Like Ann, you will be able to work as long as you wish, continuing to contribute to the cycle of income and expenditure that fuels a growing economy. You'll also be an inspiration to your children and grandchildren, proving to them that age is a state of mind.

Let me add a word of caution to balance the optimism. In large corporations, age may work against you. One day out of the blue you may be handed an early retirement notice.[5] Rather than let this happen to you, pay attention to what's going on in your company and with its competitors. The goal of every business is to survive, so be alert to trends that indicate the old way of doing business is not working anymore, which means it will not work for you either. The best way to catch the wave of the future is to think like an entrepreneur. This means you focus on satisfying clients and customers, not on your title, income, or impressing peers and upper management. Especially in today's unpredictable business world, pleasing your customer is the only way to survive.

Today (and in the future), small- to medium-sized businesses remain the engines of the economy. According to Wells Fargo Bank, 85 percent of American companies have fewer than a hundred employees. This represents 37 percent of American workers — nearly 40 million people.[6] Small, relationship-centered businesses will always be the revitalizing force in any economy, because their size allows them to respond quickly to customer needs and to changes in their niche in the marketplace. This is not the case with large and more unwieldy organizations, although they have an advantage in purchasing and distribution power.

This is also the best time in history to start your own business or individual practice, using what you know to serve others, especially those in your age group, since there are so many of you! Or perhaps you just need to reshape what you're doing so that it meets current needs. Once you complete the exercises in this book, you will know whether working for yourself or others is the way to go, and you'll know the size of the organization that is right for you. In the meantime, keep in mind that you are only one person, and you need only one job or creative opportunity.

Of course, some people are not interested in finding their passion in work. They may be wealthy, prefer to travel, volunteer, spend time with family, and take part in hobbies or other activities. Others are so unhappy with their work experiences they can't wait to retire. Or they just do not feel the desire to be creative. I urge you not to talk with these people about the process until you complete it, including family members who believe it's not possible to make money doing what you enjoy. You will have enough fear without adding their fears to yours.

Few of my clients, young or old, are aware of how distracting others' fears can be, particularly when fear is masked as criticism and competition. You may have noticed how deflated and discouraged you feel after you've been with a fearful person. When you spend time with a courageous person, on the other hand, you come away feeling hopeful about the future. You may feel upset, too, since this person will challenge your negative beliefs. Feeling upset is a normal reaction when you move out of your comfort zone. The risk you're taking may not disturb others, just as what terrifies them may be a piece of cake for you. Fear, then, is an intensely personal and often irrational experience, until you bring fear into the light of understanding.

The First Stage of Change

Identifying and facing your fears is a crucial step in the first stage of change. In his book *Think and Grow Rich*, Napoleon Hill describes six basic fears that keep you stuck in the past. These fears are as follows: the fear of poverty, the fear of criticism, the fear of loss of love, the fear of illness, the fear of old age, and the fear of death. Hill calls the six fears "ghosts," since they are often more imaginary than real.[7]

Knowing the symptoms of each fear will help you to know which fears keep you from taking the action you need to take. In the following paragraphs and throughout the book, I use the word *you* rhetorically, so interpret what I say as personal only if it applies to you.

The Fear of Poverty

Mark Twain once said about money that you either have none or not enough. The chief symptom of the fear of poverty is constantly worrying about not having enough money, even when you have the money you need (as I said, fear is not always rational). If you run mental doomsday scenarios about what will happen when you run out of money, you will become frugal to the point of miserliness. You will be obsessed with the latest get-rich-quick scheme, such as hoping to win the lottery, or with finding the magic formula for getting to the top. You will believe that if you only had more — more power, money, status, or possessions — then you would be happy. You will let people, including family members, mistreat you because you need their money. And you will envy the rich and famous.

The Fear of Criticism

If you grew up with highly critical people, any hint of disapproval can trigger the fear that you are bad, wrong, or stupid. Hypersensitivity to criticism manifests as being overly critical of others (projection); shyness and procrastination; inability to recognize when critics have the problem, not you; lack of perseverance and follow-through; inability to accept correction without defending yourself (or to accept it with gratitude); ambivalence about starting and completing projects, and about letting them go when they do not work out; hesitancy about giving honest feedback as well as praise to others; inability to confront others when they offend you; and seeing mistakes as unforgivable failures rather than as part of the creative process. Regrettably, the fear of criticism causes you to miss golden opportunities for personal and professional growth.

The Fear of Loss of Love

The symptoms of the fear of loss of love include trying to be someone you are not in order to attract affection and attention; fear of intimacy; ambivalence about commitment; serial affairs; avoidance of the responsibility (and pleasure) of close relationships; possessiveness; jealousy; clinging; spending too much time, money, and energy to get the love you crave; betraying your values; and sabotaging success to ward off the envy of people who are close to you. Like the lyrics of popular "I can't live without your love" songs, the fear of loss of love assumes that your happiness depends on someone loving and staying with you. (Happiness depends on *you* loving and staying with you, in and out of relationships.)

The Fear of Illness

This fear shows up as hypochondria (imagining you have ailments you might have but don't, or imagining that ailments you used to have will come back), self-coddling, following the latest fad diets, and avoidance of exercise (for fear you might overtax yourself). As soon as you hear the symptoms of an illness, you become sure that it is what is wrong with you. You spend time and money going to doctors only to discover that *doing* too much is making you sick. This happens because the mind is disconnected from the body, as when you value thinking over feeling, or because of misguided religious upbringing (the body is bad, so pretend it is not there). So you lose touch with the body's wisdom, how it warns you not to overeat, overwork, overextend, or use cigarettes, alcohol, or drugs to numb painful feelings. As medical studies show, all of these choices put you in the high-risk category for illness.

The Fear of Old Age

Fearing old age leads to preoccupation with and denial of age, to thinking of yourself as slipping because you are getting older, to competition with and envy of younger people, to grieving for lost youth and opportunities, and to worrying about being sick and dependent on others when you get old. The fear of old age is often based on witnessing what happened to parents or relatives who did not take care of themselves, or who were bitter and angry about getting older. If you mistreated your body when you were younger, you may have good reason to fear old age. But the body is amazingly resilient; it responds to good treatment at any age. Regular exercise, plenty of sleep, a moderate diet, meditation and prayer, a positive attitude, and doing what you love are the best antidotes to the fear of old age.

The Fear of Death

Resistance to change, hanging on to the past, hoarding, withholding praise and affection, and being stuck in boring routines all result from the fear of death. However, the most effective defense against death anxiety is to shut down emotionally, because when you don't feel anything, you live with the illusion that time is standing still. This leads you to feel that you are not getting older, and that you are not going to die someday, so there is no urgency to dive into life and love with your whole heart and soul. Sadly, you arrive at the end of your life never having lived or loved.

The fear of death and all the other fears are thieves that rob you of the joy (and challenge) of being *alive*. You can't live in the here and now because your mind is distracted by what went wrong in the past and by fear of what might go wrong in the future. The six fears often work as a team of terrorists to undermine self-confidence. Fear of old age and illness narrows your choices to a few options. Fear of criticism and poverty destroys creativity and hope. Fear of loss of love and death makes you afraid to give and receive love.

As stated previously, when we are not conscious of, or willing to admit, our fears, we project them onto "enemies." We perceive these enemies as having, or being, the problem that plagues us, such as bosses who "hold us back." In reality, it is our fear of not being a solid enough person that keeps us stuck in a rut. Once *we* know we are standing on solid ground, there are no obstacles to success.

Projection (seeing our fears and flaws in others) is active in relationships between nations and groups as well as individuals, and this leads to the need for scapegoats to blame any failures on. Denial of darker motives like envy, jealousy, cowardice, or laziness leads to an "us against them" mentality that makes peaceful relations hard to achieve and maintain, since we are essentially at war with ourselves.

If we are courageous or conscious enough to admit that what angers us about others is true about us, we bring the projection back home, which defuses the outer conflict. For example, Ann was not aware that she was afraid of the unknown. She thought she was a brave person, and she was, except when it came to letting go of control. Ann brought peace to her life when she let others learn from their choices — or not learn from them.

Naming your fears brings them out of the subconscious where they can be examined in the light of understanding. It also helps to talk with someone who has mastered the fears that trouble you. There is great comfort in expressing fear to a person who is not threatened by honesty. Once you identify your fears, ask your fears a few pointed questions. What do you think will happen to me? What do I need to do to make you feel safe? Why are you distracting me from doing what I want to do? When you put fear in the witness box, you may be surprised by what fear has to say to you.

Asking questions that begin with *what if* is another way to separate fact from fear. For example: What if I handle money well? What if I know love can't be lost? What if I'm open to criticism that helps me to improve and grow, and I ignore criticism that is wrong or harmful to me? What if I take such good care of my body that I don't think about getting ill or old? What if I cope well with my physical death when it comes? Can you see how imagining the opposite of fear (confidence) reduces fear's grip on your mind?

The Second Stage of Change

The next step is to stop what you're doing that is not working. This is not easy, because the subconscious will hold on (and hold on) until it accepts the new as logical. This means the barrier to progress is within us, not outside of us.

But you can accelerate internal change by getting rid of distractions, stuff you no longer need or use. Streamlining your surroundings will help your mind to concentrate, which in turn helps the subconscious to accept that today is not the same as yesterday. Let's start with clutter as an example of a distraction.

Clutter

When you live and work in a messy, cluttered environment, your mind is distracted by the chaos. As Karen Kingston points out in her book *Clearing Your Clutter with Feng Shui*, this is because life force (chi) gets trapped in clutter, dust, and worn-out stuff. Kingston is not talking about the normal lived-in look of a home or workspace. She is referring to the disarray that symbolizes mental stagnation. Outdated, disorderly surroundings indicate that you're stuck somewhere in the past, like those popcorn plaster ceilings that were popular in the eighties. This could be because the time period you're clinging to represents a peak experience that you don't want to leave behind or a defeat you have yet to turn to your advantage, such as a divorce or some other loss.[8]

By comparison, an environment that is clean, organized, and aesthetically pleasing needs no attention. Like a healthy body it is fine as it is, so you don't have to think about it. Your mind is free to think about *something else*. But when the something else is what you're afraid to think about, the clutter serves an unfortunate purpose.

For example, think of a risk you need to take in order to move closer to your passion. This could be as simple as making a phone call, writing an email, or talking to someone who can help you to improve. Watch to see which of the six fears rears its head as you contemplate taking action. Do you see how messy surroundings and useless belongings distract you from taking the first step into the unknown? As long as you're going to get rid of stuff *someday*, you put off taking action. Then you don't have to worry about what you will do when you fail (or succeed!). *After* you get rid of excess stuff, you will see the fear that lurked beneath the chaos. You will also know why you could not get organized.

Pruning Dead Wood

Imagine you are a gardener who needs to prune a fruit tree so that it can produce a plentiful crop in spring. The tree is your life, and the new fruit is your passion, so where is the dead wood that prevents growth? What, or who, can you remove to make room for a more bountiful life?

You probably feel tired just thinking about the task ahead of you. Perhaps it brings to mind the last time you tried to trim down your life. Did you throw stuff away or did you just shift it around? Were you aware of the anxiety you felt when you thought about letting go of certain items and relationships? Did you stop in the middle of the project and put it off to another day? Did you get rid of things only to acquire more stuff? Did you allow people to stay in your life in order to avoid the responsibility for ending those relationships?

Having passion in midlife and beyond as your goal this time will motivate you to complete the pruning process. Begin by walking through your house or apartment, then your garage or storage space. If your environment is already clean, clutter free, and updated, just read the rest of the chapter, using suggestions that apply to you.

Make a list of the things you can get rid of right away. If you prefer, make a minimum and a maximum list, what you know you will get to now, and what you will get to later. Both lists are likely to include items that belong to your children, grandchildren, relatives, and friends. Next, call everybody to arrange a pickup date.

If you feel reluctant to ask people to come and get their stuff, remember that guilt comes up frequently during the second stage of change. This is because, when you change, you are announcing that what you used to do was wrong, and this stirs up resentment in some people and leads to your feelings of guilt.

When you aren't aware that people are resentful, you may conclude there is something wrong with you when they get upset with you. If these people are honest enough to say, "I feel resentful; I wish I had the courage to do what you're doing," this brings resentment out into the open where it can be discussed and laughed about.

If you are married or living with someone, you will want to ask your partner to help with the streamlining project. If your partner refuses to cooperate or sabotages your efforts, you will need to take a hard look at this relationship. The most painful part of personal growth is the end of relationships you thought would last forever. If there are no other alternatives, it's best to take responsibility for ending what is over. Otherwise you prolong the inevitable, or you set things up so that the other person leaves you. Then you not only feel like a Victim but you also lose an opportunity for growth.

Happily, after initial resistance, and when the uncomfortable stage of change is over, many people get excited about change for the better. In Ann's case, once her husband and teenagers were sure the new worked better than the old, they copied Ann's brave example.

The Three-Piles Technique

To start the clearing process, begin with your bathroom, since that's the smallest room in the house. The bathroom is also a symbol of cleansing and elimination, so this aspect fits right into what you're doing. If you have more than one bathroom, clear one room at a time, using the three-piles technique. The first pile contains what you never use and will throw away. The second pile is what you will donate or give away. The third pile is what you love and always use. Remind yourself that this is the first step to finding your passion.

Now, remove everything from your bathroom — yes, *everything* except the toilet, sink, and tub, unless these need replacing. Separate items into the three piles: items you never use and will throw away; items someone else can use; and items you love and always use.

Once everything is out of the bathroom, give the room and cabinets a thorough cleaning. If the room needs painting, choose soothing colors. Repair leaky faucets, add new caulking on the tub or shower, add tile on the floor, and install up-to-date fixtures, shelves, and cabinets, if needed. Put in new shelf lining, candles, and soap, and new or freshly washed towels, bath mat, and shower curtain, if needed. Think of the atmosphere you want to create in the space where you cleanse and groom yourself: do the colors and textures reflect who you are and what you value?

Next, put back what you *love and always use*. Now put the *never use/throwaway* pile in the trash and store the *never use/donate* pile in boxes in the garage or storage space. You will add to these boxes as you go through each room in your house or apartment.

Now, empty your bedroom. If you have more than one bedroom, start with the smallest one. If you need help moving the furniture, ask a friend or hire a person with a strong back and shoulders. After the furniture is removed, clean the windows, window coverings, and the floor or carpet. If needed, paint the room in a quiet, restful color.

Then take all the items out of the drawers and place them in three piles. Again, pile one contains what you never use and will throw away, pile two what you do not use but can donate, and pile three what you love and always use and will keep.

If your mattress and box spring are worn out, buy a new set. The mattress store will remove your old set when they deliver your new mattress. Throw away old bedding items and replace them with new pillows, sheets, and blankets in matching colors or prints.

Empty all your closets, again using the three-piles technique. Maybe that dress or jacket or those shoes looked great ten years ago, but they are out of style and need to go. Be ruthless. If you have not worn it in a year, out it goes — put it in the throwaway or the donate pile. Keep in mind that your authentic self knows what to throw or give away, although you will not know that for sure until those belongings are gone.

Be sure to use the three-piles technique with your closet shelves, since they are magnets for stuff you have had for years and years but never use. Buy new matching plastic hangers, shoe stands, or hanging bags, and plastic storage boxes or baskets you can label for items you *love and always use*. Then your closet will look fresh and up-to-date, like you.

You will probably go through the three-piles process more than once in some rooms. After a few days, weeks, or even months, you may decide to discard stuff you thought you wanted to keep. Good for you. Just put those items in the throwaway or donate piles.

If you can afford it, hire a professional organizer to help you wrap up the project or, as I said earlier, ask a friend or relative to help you. Coming down the home stretch with someone whose company you enjoy is a great deal of fun. When you're done, you can help her clear the clutter from *her* life. Or you can treat her to dinner and a movie or give her a special gift.

Now we move on to your kitchen. Oh boy, you say, this is going to take forever. Nowhere is there likely to be more clutter than in the kitchen, especially in kitchen junk drawers. You might as well start by emptying the kitchen drawers and separating their contents into three piles: *never use/throw away, never use/donate*, and *love/always use/keep*. No, you don't need two spatulas and three frying pans, and since the kids are gone, you don't need extra-large boxes of food and jumbo-size containers. You will never use twenty drying towels; one for every other day will do. Donate that extra set of dishes, and give all those cookbooks to your favorite cooks, unless cooking turns out to be your passion.

Clean the kitchen and, if needed, paint it before you put back the items you *love and always use*. Yes, you will have some empty shelves. Do not fill them up. Let them be. If you can resist the urge to fill empty space, you have passed the first test in finding your passion. Yes, you will feel strange. But strange is better than distracted.

Complete the clearing process in all the other rooms in your house or apartment. Always ask yourself, "Do I love it? Do I use it?" This will help you get rid of chairs, tables, couches, lamps, knickknacks, collections, videos, tapes, CDs, and memorabilia. Similarly, if you have a home office or den, discard furniture, supplies, paper, and files until all that is left is what you *use and love*. You may want to replace your desktop computer with a laptop that takes up less space.

Take frequent breaks after you discard stuff to allow time for your mind and emotions to adjust to the changes you're making. If you're like most people, you underestimate the time needed to assimilate change, the sorting, mulling-over process so necessary for clear thinking. Instead, you probably go right on to the next experience and then wonder why you feel so scattered.

Depending on the size of your house or apartment and the amount of clutter, the clearing process can take weeks or even months. But time is going to go by anyway, so you might as well make good use of it. Just think, you will never have to do this again. All you will need to do is maintain your minimalist lifestyle.

As you near the end of the elimination project, set a date for a garage sale of the *never use/donate* items. This will give you a deadline to get the project done. Otherwise, you'll procrastinate or, worse, keep stuff. You can use the proceeds to pay for paint, shelves, or other organizing needs, not more stuff! If you don't want to have a garage sale, you can give stuff away to friends, relatives, and neighbors, call your favorite local charity to pick up these items, or take them to Goodwill Industries or Salvation Army donation sites.

Now empty your garage or storage space. Again, use the three-piles technique. Before you put anything back in the garage, give it a good cleaning. Put up shelves to keep items you *love/always use* off the floor.

Next, clear your car of clutter, including stuff in the glove compartment and trunk. Take the car to a car wash to have it washed and vacuumed, or get the car detailed by a professional. If your car needs servicing or repair, take it to an expert. Your car symbolizes the way you get around in life. Driving a clean, well-running vehicle indicates that you know where you're going and why.

With all the clutter out of your surroundings, you'll be able to see what else makes you feel so tired you can't do what you want to do. These distractions can include people who take advantage of you or whose negativity and poor judgment empty your energy supply and wallet.

People Distractions

Some people accuse you of being selfish when you do what you want to do. Or is it *you* who feels selfish when you take care of your needs? Perhaps you are afraid you'll fail at what you want to do, so you allow, even court, distractions. Maybe you believe it's noble to sacrifice your time,

money, and energy for others: coworkers, subordinates, bosses, customers, clients, and grown-up children who prolong adolescence with
their dependence on you, or friends and family members who complain
but don't do anything about their problems.

Misplaced compassion or naïveté about the dark side of human nature compels you to extend sympathy, when what people need from you
is thoughtful confrontation. But the fear of criticism and its younger
sibling, the fear of failure, cause you to act against your best interests.
Giving too much is a symptom of the fear of loss of love. When you
grow up with people who are long on criticism and short on support,
you try to please them to get the love you need and deserve. This strategy works initially, which is why you repeat it. But then comes the inevitable letdown when others do not respond in kind. Ah, you think,
disappointment must be my lot in life.

Disillusionment will be your lot in life until you accept that some
people do not want to do the work it takes to truly love another person,
and that this choice has nothing to do with you. Remember the power
of the past? You go back to what you know because it's familiar, even
though it causes you to feel pain. Subconsciously, *not* getting your needs
met is what you expect.

A need is something that is essential to your well-being, such as
safety, solitude, friendship, and communication. When these needs are
met, you feel content, as when you've had a satisfying meal. But if you
believe you are not supposed to have needs (as people do when their
self-esteem is low), you always put others' needs first. Then you don't
feel selfish; you feel angry and resentful. Now you're back in familiar
territory.

It is noble and even spiritual to put others' needs first; in fact, the
secret of happiness lies in serving others. But giving is the most subtle
ego game of all when motives are not truly selfless. In other words, only
a well-nourished self can nourish others. Otherwise, you give to get
something back. The other person picks up on your ulterior motive and
holds back what you need (gotcha).

You will know you're on the right track when you give without expecting a return, and when you don't feel used. Before you give away time, money, or energy, determine your motives: Are they truly selfless, or are you giving because you feel sorry for someone? Do you feel guilty? Do you want something in return: approval, gratitude, or some other quid pro quo?

Again, the paradox of change is that healthy choices feel awkward and wrong, whereas self-destructive choices, such as staying with hurtful people, feel right because they are known. You rationalize mistreatment by telling yourself, "It's not that bad," "I should be able to handle this," "I'm being too judgmental," or "I shouldn't be feeling this way." The truth is, you *do* feel that way and with good reason, but you're afraid that if you leave, others will get angry and retaliate. Or that you will discover they don't really care about you, that all they care about is what they get from you, which is why you want to leave.

It's painful to admit that people use you for their selfish purposes. You feel foolish and betrayed. You wonder how you could have been so blind. Rather than castigate yourself, ask why you got involved with these people in the first place. What need (security, love, friendship) did you hope to fill? Understanding your motivation prevents you from turning back once you learn to fill that need in healthier ways.

Paying too much attention to what's going on in the world is another way to distract yourself from your fears. It's good to be an involved citizen, but trying to save, or condemn, the world when your life needs attention is not the best use of your time. Be assured, when your inner world is in order you will help the world.

Remember, the first stage of change is admitting that what you are doing isn't working. It doesn't work to blind yourself to others' selfish motives, to say one thing and then do another, or to feel guilty when you take care of your needs, unless *not* achieving your heart's desire is your objective. What works is to hold still and look at your fears without judgment. When your mind is quiet, you'll hear the voice that wants the best for you and for everyone else. Yes, you will feel uncomfortable with what your authentic self wants to do, but you won't feel resentful.

If you hang in there and accept the anxiety that accompanies the middle stage of change, time will prove you made the right decision. The people who care about you will be happy for you even when they don't have your full attention. Some will be inspired by your brave example. Those who care only about themselves will leave your life and move on to their next Victim.

Emotional Distractions

You will have mixed emotions about getting rid of stuff that symbolizes outmoded parts of your personality. One of my clients held on to a wardrobe she bought when she worked as a designer for a large retail corporation. Her closet looked a great deal like her mind, full of confusion and clutter (yes, occasionally I go on field trips). At the time we met, Julie didn't know her values were changing, and this led to her conflicts with bosses at work. (I discuss values in chapter 5.) Chronic fatigue was just one symptom of forcing herself to do what she didn't want to do, as was her elevated blood pressure.

While Julie was writing her life story (again, the first assignment I give to my clients), she realized that her mother, Jane, used her children to satisfy emotional needs not being met in her marriage. She expected the children to provide the love she craved, which was also true about Jane's mother, Alice, and so on, all the way back to the first unhappy woman in the family line. When a woman (or man) does not dare to live her life, she compensates by living through the lives of her children, or through the life of someone she would like to be but is too fearful to emulate. For example, Julie's mother wanted recognition but was afraid to risk exposure — and this points to the fear of criticism.

Vicarious living is fair when we pay for it by attending concerts and exhibits, by buying books and art, and by watching movies, videos, and sports events. But living through others' creativity places a heavy and unfair burden on them, especially on children, who want their parents to be happy and, at the same time, deeply resent their intrusiveness.

Many people find it hard to express uncomfortable emotions to their parents and, in some cases, to admit that their parents were not capable of love. Instead, they displace their anger and resentment about not getting what they needed from their parents onto their children: the "sins" of one generation are passed down to the next.

It took courage for Julie to admit that she felt angry with her grandmother, Alice, and her mother, Jane. It took even more courage to admit that she allowed them to cross her boundaries because she believed she was not supposed to have needs, although her subconscious desires told a different story (how's that for a recipe for conflict?). She had just kept working harder, like the overly trusting horse in George Orwell's *Animal Farm* that wound up in the glue factory.

Julie's authentic self longed to break free from the repressive family script, but since she didn't *feel* anger, she didn't know she *was* angry when she gave away too much time and energy. Instead, her blood pressure rose and she felt tired all the time. This is an example of how life scripts — stories that always end in failure — are passed down through the generations, in this case, from grandmother to mother to daughter.

Chronic fatigue is the normal reaction when people don't get the solitude they need to recharge their mental and emotional batteries. This is particularly true for introverts like Julie, who are the minority in Western cultures, where people get charged up around other people. People both need to be with others and need to be alone; what works for each person is a matter of degree. If you are on the extrovert end of the scale, you like to be around people about 60 to 80 percent of the time and alone the rest of the time. If you are an introvert the reverse ratio is true: you need to be alone about 60 to 80 percent of the time, and the remaining time you are comfortable with others. When your work and relationships accommodate these boundaries, you feel centered and grounded. You can see why introverts like Julie frequently feel there is something wrong with them when they can't keep up with extroverts, and why extroverts feel rejected by introverts when the latter want to be alone.

When you add grandparents' and parents' compensating behavior to the mix, it's not surprising that overstimulation is the norm in the Western world. The inner life that needs to be developed, particularly when we reach midlife, is rejected for a more youthful and exhausting stage. The strife in the world, then, mirrors the strife within.

As Julie worked on changing her script (an outline for how to do this is in the next chapter), she realized she was repeating her mother and grandmother's "I have to take care of everybody and I'm mad as heck about it" scripts. Feeling burdened and being secretly mad about it is a script I've noticed in most of the autobiographies I read. These stories are a microcosm of a larger societal dilemma: the rejection of intuition as a way to solve problems. Holding still and looking inward for solutions to problems is not the accepted strategy. Instead you hear, "You need to get out there and circulate," as though the information you need is "out there."

Meeting with others can help you clarify your values. For example, you find a job, a business, or a relationship. But soon you discover that you're up against the same old problems, and you're exhausted from trying to make work what will never work for you. Even so, it's more comfortable to feel exhausted than it is to feel the anxiety that comes up when you hold still.

Feelings of transgression and guilt, and the fear of punishment, are inherent in the struggle to become an authentic person. You can expect an upsurge of terror from your subconscious when you break free from parental, societal, and religious injunctions about how to behave and what to believe. Even insignificant choices can stir up the fear that you will be thrown out on the tundra with the big woolies. This is because the primal part of the brain is programmed to align with the group for protection against danger, the first group being the family. Too much individuality leads to anarchy and even death. However, too much conformity to the group leads to stagnation and decay, the feeling of staleness you have when you're stuck in a rut. Society and families need brave individuals to shake up the status quo with constructive rebellion. Since these men and women represent change for the better, they threaten those who cling to the past.

Julie shook up the status quo when she decided that many people can and want to solve their problems (a logical conclusion). Those who don't want to do so need to learn there are no free rides. Leaving behind the role of the Rescuer dissolved the anger Julie felt about being used. She accepted that it was up to her to draw the line and to absorb the guilt that accompanies departure from family conditioning. She was excited about the changes she was making, although it was months before she felt comfortable whenever she withdrew to take care of her needs. Her old guilt about being selfish kept intruding like an unwanted visitor, causing her to backslide into old behavior. But the voices of her mother and grandmother got quieter and quieter over time, eventually diminishing to whispers that Julie ignored.

Julie is an example of a person who knows something intellectually, but who, until she knows it emotionally, repeats the past. By "knows it emotionally," I'm referring to the moment when one's subconscious mind accepts the new as true. This maddeningly entrenched part of the psyche wants proof before it lets go of old ways of thinking and relating — with good reason, since life is unstable when you change your mind all the time.

Subconsciously, Julie had believed she could not survive doing what she loved. To convince her subconscious that it was logical to make money doing what she enjoyed, she repeated the following sentence several times a day: "I am *comfortable* getting paid to do the work I love, at my own pace and in my own way." Using the word *comfortable* helped her subconscious to stop feeling comfortable with what was familiar: hating work but forcing herself to do it for the money. After repeating this sentence for about three weeks, Julie noticed a shift in her thinking. "Now I see that the way I thought about work and money held me back," she told me (a breakthrough!).

Julie moved into the final stage of change when she decided to work from home as an independent designer. She and her husband sold their large home and bought a less expensive house for Julie to remodel. Transforming older houses into updated, energy-efficient homes had long been a goal of hers. This is an example of the creative process: one small step leads to greater steps.

It took time for Julie's dream of working independently to become a reality, but she and her husband began by reducing their debt and accumulating enough savings to live on for a year. After she left her job, Julie donated her wardrobe to a group that helped women put their best foot forward in job interviews. "I get exhausted just thinking about those clothes," Julie said when we met in my home office. "Up at dawn, going to meeting after meeting after meeting all day long, and hurrying to catch planes to faraway places. The only design time I had was on weekends. But I truly believed I'd fail if I worked for myself," she added. "And I would have had I not taken the small steps that got me where I am. Going slowly gave my subconscious time to adjust to thinking like an entrepreneur."

Today, Julie dresses, lives, and works in her own way and at her own pace, rather than as an overdressed, long-suffering martyr. And yes, her blood pressure has dropped. "Being me is so simple," Julie sighed. "No wonder I had so many physical ailments — chronic this and chronic that. I spent thousands of dollars on health care when my body was telling me that I needed to work by myself. I don't know why it took me so long to see the obvious."

"The truth is always obvious once we see it," I said, smiling.

Like Julie, you will experience a symbolic death when you let go of old ways of thinking. You may even have dreams of death and destruction. Don't be alarmed when this happens. Upheaval dreams indicate that you're in the middle stage of change. To repeat, change is uncomfortable. Just when you think you're moving forward, you go back to what's familiar. Don't be angry with yourself when this happens. Once your subconscious accepts the new as better than the old, your dreams will reflect the calm that follows the winds of change.

Physical Distractions

Feelings move more slowly than thoughts, so don't rush your feelings. Give yourself all the time you need to feel and understand them. When I say *feelings* I am not referring to the times when you're anxious and out of control. That chaotic state of mind is usually the result of *denying* your feelings. Perhaps an event or person triggers an inferiority complex, as when you take a medical test or go on a date or an interview. When the test, date, or interview is over and you pass, you realize your fear was groundless.

Few of us are taught how feelings work or what feelings are for, unless we express feeling in our work. We learn from an early age to dismiss, intellectualize, or ignore our feelings, particularly feelings like anger and anxiety, which often get displaced and take the form of physical pain, according to Dr. John E. Sarno, the author of *Healing Back Pain: The Mind-Body Connection.*[9]

Dr. Sarno says that most back pain is not structural, meaning that there is nothing wrong with the back, although the pain can be excruciating. The physical discomfort is caused by mild oxygen deprivation in muscles, a result of tension that comes from displaced anger and anxiety. Typically, those who suffer from what Dr. Sarno calls tension myositis syndrome are conscientious, hardworking people who feel burdened but are too guilty to protest (does this sound like Julie?). Their competence magnetizes other people who expect the hard worker to make life easy for them, which in turn causes the back pain sufferer to feel resentful.

According to Dr. Sarno, we program the brain at an early age to displace anger and anxiety and transform it into socially acceptable physical pain, such as backaches, headaches, heartaches, asthma, and gastrointestinal and other ailments. Even burns, fevers, infections, and accidents are ways the body expresses anger and anxiety.

Until recently most doctors viewed the body as separate from the mind, a legacy of the seventeenth-century French mathematician and philosopher René Descartes ("I am thinking therefore I exist"). As often happens in history, Cartesian rationality was a pendulum swing away from the skepticism that had followed the Protestant revolution, a time when change and its companion, doubt, had been in full force.[10] Descartes said, "Certainty is the key to knowledge." And the only thing he was certain of was that he thought about his experiences. Descartes was a brilliant logician, but it would have been better for all of us had he accepted feeling as an equally valid way to interpret experience.

His discounting of the value of feeling is probably why Descartes' peers described him as cold and selfish, common characteristics of people whose intellect holds sway. You need thinking to connect the dots between cause and effect, but to connect your heart to your actions you need to feel. Sarno says the emphasis on thinking and the exclusion of feeling causes many doctors to misdiagnose physical ailments. Reprogramming the brain to eliminate physical pain, instead of using scientifically proven methods like surgery or medication, sounds like voodoo to them. Before Dr. Sarno's patients came to him, their doctors treated their pain as the result of inflammation or structural damage, when neither was the source of the problem. Sarno says this is not unusual; the health care industry consumes billions of dollars every year treating the physical symptoms of emotional pain.

Education and awareness are the keys to permanent recovery from the symptoms of tension myositis syndrome, Sarno says, an insight he gained from his own experience. Like many in the caregiving professions, Sarno worked too hard and then displaced how he felt about being overwhelmed, and so developed psychosomatic ailments, until his intuition made the leap that cured him and his patients. Just *knowing* physical pain is not structural shifted Sarno's patients' thinking to a psychological point of view, which reprogrammed the brain. Once his patients became aware that they were angry or anxious, there was no need for the brain to send those emotions into the body. In the majority of cases, symptoms went away and stayed away without therapy.[11]

To test Dr. Sarno's mind-body correlation, the next time you experience physical pain that does not have a structural or organic cause, ask if you are angry or anxious about something. Are you suppressing feelings because of one or more of the six basic fears: the fear of poverty, criticism, loss of love, illness, old age, or death? What part of your body is expressing anger and anxiety? What does this area of the body symbolize? For example, chest pain could be an emotional injury. Pain in the reproductive organs might be blocked creativity. Leg pain could indicate fear of moving forward. Back pain would be anxiety about not being supported financially or emotionally. Is the pain a pattern that began in childhood or adolescence?

When Julie was a girl, she felt angry and anxious because of her father's violent temper and her mother's acquiescence to his authority. Julie was too young to leave the situation and too frightened to speak up, so she displaced how she felt, developing sore throats and overeating. Looking at the past with clear-eyed objectivity helped Julie to see that her mother, Jane, had felt anger and anxiety just as Julie did. Jane had been afraid of her husband, but had needed his income to support her and the children. Because she couldn't leave, Jane drowned her sorrow in alcohol. Her suppression of her painful feelings gave rise to a judgmental attitude toward women who expressed anger and anxiety (this is an example of projection), including toward Julie when she expressed these emotions.

To make matters more complicated, Julie's beloved grandmother, Alice, also disapproved of female anger, but not of male anger. Alice was the product of religious beliefs that said men were superior to women, and at the same time, that men could not control themselves. Women, on the other hand, were better than that, an irrational conclusion that flowed down through the generations like water over a dam. Looking at Alice as a person rather than as an all-powerful authority figure — a child's point of view — altered the way Julie thought of her grandmother and herself. Once Alice's erroneous assumptions about gender were excised from Julie's mind, she was able to say no without feeling guilty and yes to what was best for her.

Julie also signed up for karate and yoga classes to get out of her head and into her body. Karate showed her how to be assertive; yoga helped her to listen to her body. In time and with practice, she knew when she *felt* anger and what to do about it. Then her physical pain disappeared.

Like Julie, you can stop your body from reacting physically to painful emotions. Talk to your brain; yell at it if need be, Dr. Sarno says. When tension myositis syndrome kicks in, don't be intimidated by the pain. Tell yourself that the pain is a harmless condition caused by muscles that are tense from lack of oxygen. Let yourself know what you are angry or anxious about, and then do something about it. Feeling anger and anxiety in their early stages, before they escalate to rage and panic, nips misunderstandings in the bud. While you're in a rational frame of mind, you can say what you think in a neutral tone of voice. You will also hear what others say to you.

An added benefit of emotional honesty is that you will have more empathy for others' painful feelings, which makes you a better communicator. Your body will be happier too, since it won't have to get sick or injured as a result of your mind's attempt to get your attention.

The Third Stage of Change

Here you are at last, in the third and final stage of change. You faced your fears head on, seeing them as challenges to overcome rather than as excuses to procrastinate. Then you eliminated (or are in the process of eliminating) distractions from your life: clutter, obsolete stuff, and the tendency to feel guilty about not wanting to spend time with people who drain your energy. Now that you know keeping busy was a way to avoid your fears, you set aside time every day to work through fears and to process your thoughts and feelings. To keep your mind, body, and spirit in good shape, you exercise, eat, and drink moderately and you get plenty of sleep. Rather than displace anger and anxiety and transform it into physical ailments, you tell your brain that you want to feel these feelings so that you know what to do and what not to do.

Simplifying your life allows you to think about what is important to you at this stage of life: finding the niche where you will grow to your full potential and make the money you need. When you relapse into old habits, you turn around and face your fears again and again, until nothing can tempt you to go back to the past.

If you need help, you select advisors whose lives demonstrate what they say, as opposed to people who talk a good game but don't live it. You avoid advisors who follow a guru's lead, or who try to be all things to all people.

When you wake up in the morning, all you see is what you love and use. You feel so light and free you wonder why it took you so long to start the elimination process. You may even decide to move to a smaller, less demanding space. Or you may just walk around your surroundings feeling amazed by how different life feels. When passion in midlife and beyond is your goal, less is definitely more.

SUMMARY

1. Face your fears head on.
2. Throw away or donate what you do not use.
3. Keep only what you love and use.
4. Persevere through the difficult middle stage of change.
5. Celebrate the new, streamlined you.

CHAPTER 3

Rewrite Your Life Story

Study the past if you would divine the future.
— CONFUCIUS

N ow that you have eliminated the distractions from your life (well, most of them), you are ready to take the next step to finding your perfect niche: rewrite your life story to reflect the desires of your authentic self, the core of your personality, which wants to live the rest of life to the fullest. Ahead is an outline that will help you organize the story in sections, with questions that prompt awareness of the choices that worked and the choices that did not work, some of which you may still repeat.

Choices that work are made in a calm state of mind at the right stages of life. If you grew up in a relatively stable environment, you gathered and sorted through information before making decisions. You felt free at any time to change your mind to adapt to new information and circumstances. This open, flexible attitude carried forward into adult life, which you experience with spontaneity and liveliness.

By contrast, if you grew up in an alcoholic, neglectful, violent, controlling, overly religious, or overly sexualized family, you were so preoccupied with keeping the chaos at bay that you couldn't think clearly, listen to your feelings, consider the consequences before you acted, change your mind, or trust your intuition. In fact when you were honest, your parents or other caretakers may have criticized, punished, ridiculed, or abandoned you. Like most children, you blamed yourself, or you copied your parents' behavior, or you expressed how you felt in self-destructive ways. If you concluded that this outcome was your destiny, then this set the course of your life on a downward spiral, according to psychotherapist Claude Steiner, the author of *Games Alcoholics Play*.[1]

Becoming aware of when and under what circumstances you concluded that your story was not going to turn out well gives you the power to change that decision. The more you understand the influence of the past on the present situation and accept it emotionally as well as intellectually, the more control you have over inner conflicts and your ability to resolve them.

At first, you will feel reluctant to write about the past. All those mistakes. All that pain! But once you get into the story, you will be fascinated (passion clue) by what you learn, not only about yourself but also about every other character in the story. Looking at family members (and yourself) as though they were characters in a novel will give you a new way to think about the past. Suddenly, relatives become people rather than authority figures you idealize, fear, or rebel against. If you use first names for your grandparents and parents, you'll have even more objectivity about what was going on (what was *really* going on) between and among yourself and your family members.

Objectivity is the ability to assess people and situations without being influenced by emotion or prejudice. This is impossible to do when you use charged words like *mother (mom)*, *father (dad)*, *grandfather*, *grandmother*, *sister*, *brother*, and words that end with *in-law*. Family attachment makes it hard to see these people as they are, rather than as you want, need, or imagine them to be. As an experiment, think of your grandparents and parents by their first names, as if you were not related to them. How do you feel when you do this? Disrespectful? Frightened? Liberated? Are you angry with me for even suggesting the idea? Or do you see what you could not see before?

How would you feel if your adult children and grandchildren called you by your first name? Would you be pleased to know they think of you as a person? Or would you feel a sense of loss? Would they understand why you wanted them to think of you as an individual and not only as a relative? If not, can you see how their need for security keeps you in a role that is stifling to your authentic self?

I am not suggesting that people stop using words like *mother, father, grandfather, grandmother, daughter,* and *son,* and so on. After all, these words are the glue that holds civilization and families together. But these same words can be used to control others. For example: "I'm your mother and don't you forget it! Just look at all I've done for you." Or when you set limits, you might hear, "Why don't you ever call your sister? She just got out of drug rehab again and she needs your attention." Or as one client's father shouted when his daughter said she didn't think of him as her father anymore, "Who am I if I'm not your father?"

Who indeed? No genuine bond of love is threatened by objectivity. On the contrary, love blossoms in an atmosphere of freedom. Otherwise, what passes for love is mutual dependence, each party manipulating the other to get what he or she wants.

As you may know, there is a direct correlation between dependence and hostility. The more dependent you are, the more hostile you feel toward what or whom you are dependent on, and toward those who threaten your dependency — witness the people who fight over power, money, property, not getting their emotional needs met, and addictions.

It's good to be able to depend on people and for them to be able to depend on you. But a dependency is anything or anyone you believe you can't live without. Then, what you depend on dominates your life, which is why so much fear and defensiveness surround a dependency. If you depend on your job for your identity and you are fired, you feel hostile toward your boss. If you are dependent on drugs, cigarettes, alcohol, food, or stuff, you feel hostile toward what you depend on, and you feel hostile toward anyone who confronts you with the addiction.

Happily, there is also a correlation between respect and independence. The healthier and more independent individuals are, the greater the chance for respectful boundaries and resolution of conflict. Both parties can make it alone, but they choose to associate for mutual benefit: love, shared journeys, and so on. When problems arise, they talk them through until both sides' needs are met.

Subjectivity, on the other hand, obscures the other's point of view. Looking at the world from the inside out is necessary in order to tap the imagination for original thoughts and ideas, as all artists and other creative people know. But to get to the facts of any situation, especially family scripts, you have to look from the outside in, observing what *is* without flinching or judging.

However, life scripts are hard to identify, because they are what you take for granted as truth: the sun rises in the morning, and Halloween falls on the last day of October. As Steiner says, scripts that you assume to be true compel you to make the same choices throughout life, until you are so tired of failure you will do whatever it takes to change.[2]

Steiner's work is based on transactional analysis theory pioneered by Eric Berne, the author of the classic book *Games People Play*.[3] Like his mentor, Steiner gained his insights while observing the games patients played to get their needs met. "Games are a series of transactions with a covert motive and a payoff," Steiner says. "They are the medium in which people obtain strokes."[4] Strokes are exchanges between people that meet stimulation needs, such as the need for touch, attention, and praise. When needs are not met positively, Steiner says, people cause trouble, get ill, or get drunk, since a negative stroke is better than none. So, if parents pay attention to their children when they cause trouble and ignore them when they do well, the children will learn to fail in order to get attention. Later in life, this pattern is hard to change because they believe if they solve their problems no one will pay attention to them; there will be no strokes.

Giving and receiving negative strokes is typical in marriages where one partner needs affection and the other partner withholds affection as a way to stay in control. The emotionally starved partner tries hard, and then harder, to get stimulation needs met. When that doesn't work, the only option left is to cause trouble, to have affairs, drink, do drugs, or express rage. A child in such a family identifies with the parent of choice. It's clear that "monkey see, monkey do" does not just apply to primates who live in trees.

Children of withholding parents often conclude that they are not supposed to have needs or that they are not good enough to warrant affection. Simultaneously they conclude that the adults for whom they are not good enough *are* good enough (see the faulty logic?). Then these children spend the rest of their lives trying to get the approval of withholding people who remind them of their parents. It doesn't occur to them to ask themselves if they approve of people who withhold, since that would change the script.

Growing up with warring parents is similar to what soldiers experience in combat. Since their primary need is to survive, soldiers have to be hypervigilant for enemies hiding behind every rock and tree. They can't relax and let down their guard; if they do they could lose their lives. According to Dr. Jonathan Shay, the author of *Odysseus in America: Combat Trauma and the Trials of Homecoming*, the combat environment inflicts psychological injuries that can do more damage than physical injuries, since emotional wounds are hidden because of shame or embarrassment.[5]

Dr. Shay compares Homer's description of Odysseus's feelings of alienation after the Trojan War with the postwar trauma felt by American veterans. Many of these brave men and women assume there is something wrong with them when they have nightmares, emotional ups and downs, sleep and nervous disorders, troubled relationships, and other symptoms of psychological injury, when the truth is that every combat veteran is damaged by exposure to war. Shay says one solution is for leaders at the unit level to prepare soldiers to accept emotional injury as normal and to encourage them to get help once they arrive home. He suggests that veterans talk with other combat veterans as a way to process what they witnessed on the battlefield. He says peers are often more helpful than mental health professionals who have not experienced war. The good news is that today's veterans are writing books about their combat experiences. Others are forming support groups via the Internet to talk about their thoughts and feelings. Many veterans are discovering that asking for help does not mean they are weak; it means they are smart.

If you grew up in a combat zone, you may feel ashamed or embarrassed when you feel scared and vulnerable. You may think you should be able to handle everything by yourself. To change this illogical conclusion, talk with sympathetic listeners and write about what you went through, since writing distances you from past events. When you can see the value of the past, no matter how painful, your mind and heart are whole again.

A Script Is a Generalization

Mental clarity is the ability to make distinctions between the false and the true, between what passes for love and genuine love. Mental confusion is based on generalizations you believe are true about everyone. You can recognize a generality whenever you hear someone say, "That's just the way men [or women] are." Imagine a girl who is twelve years old when her mother tells her that every man has a wandering eye and that he will have sexual relations with other women. That doesn't mean he loves them, the mother hastens to add; he loves his wife, but that's just the way men are.

Based on her mother's "that's just the way men are" script, what would the daughter conclude about men? Men are untrustworthy. Women are sex objects. What would challenge these generalizations? Realizing that her mother rationalizes her husband's behavior because she is financially dependent on him. Then the daughter can make the money she needs and meet a man who values intimacy.

Another conclusion you may have made when you were too young to know what you were doing is "People won't like me if I excel." To avoid the dislike, teasing, and criticism that can go with standing out from the group, you downplayed your gifts. This decision kept you out of the limelight, but it also set you up for underachievement. Ironically, you envy those who do their best. The decision to not do your best because of your fear of being envied or disliked is illogical, since not all people envy or dislike people who display excellence; many admire and emulate them. However, people do gossip about you when you are interesting — namely, family members, neighbors, writers for the *National Enquirer* and *People* magazine, radio and television talk show hosts, and Internet bloggers. As an adult you know that gossip and envy go with the territory of success. Some people dislike and envy you; some adore you; others are inspired by your example. But when you are young, your mind is not developed enough to make these logical distinctions.

Another premature decision made under pressure is that people reject you when you are honest. The question that challenges this or any generalization is "What people am I referring to?" Or "Who specifically rejects me when I am honest?" Are you talking about wishy-washy parents, siblings, friends, a spouse, partner, coworker, boss, or (gasp) your own wishy-washy self? Would you want these people on your side in a pinch? If not, why do you care about what fearful folks think of you? Probably because you don't see them as fearful.

Youth lacks the experience that tests the validity of what people say. And most of what children know is based on a limited sample of information — the family. When you question adults and they deny your perceptions, you assume they must be right, rather than say to yourself, "These people are nuts, and I can hardly wait to get out of here."

Unless you know to bide your time, or you express rebellion in constructive ways, such as by using your talent and brains to get validation *outside* the family, you lose touch with the authentic self, which leaves you feeling isolated and alone. You don't have to be an Academy Award–winning actor to know how to perpetuate this script.

"I'm worthless" is another script that is formed in reaction to the way you are treated by family members. Let's say your father was verbally abusive, and because of this you concluded you were worthless. This is an illogical conclusion, because verbally abusive people mistreat everyone to mask their own feelings of inferiority. As a child you were not aware that your father felt inferior and that this had nothing to do with you (children are highly subjective). Nor did you know that, most likely, he had been the target of *his* father's feelings of inferiority, who'd had the same experience with *his* father, and so on, all the way back to the first father in the family's history who felt inferior.[6]

Since you loved your father and you depended on him for survival, what he said about you stuck in your young mind like glue to a clean surface. Later your bond (as in *bondage*) to him attracted men who confirmed your "I'm worthless" script (certainly you were worthless to them!). Remember, your brain is hardwired to repeat what you know, even though this causes you to feel pain. This is why children will not leave abusive parents even when offered a safe, loving home.

How do you change a self-destructive script? By seeing your father (use his first name here) exactly as he is, not as you want him to be. Giving up the idealized view of your father that you had as a child feels like a loss, but what you gain is the ability to see him from an adult's perspective. Then you can disagree with him and other men who remind you of him. The ability to make this distinction allows you to see the men who treat you and others with courtesy and respect.

Susan's Story

"I realize now that my father was not as smart as I thought he was," Susan wrote in the conclusion of her autobiography. "He has a PhD, but he is emotionally immature. After I wrote about my grandfather, I realized that my father is just like him: both have to be the center of attention."

Susan's father, Jim, was an engineer who wanted to be a writer and philosopher, but he could not take criticism. Since humility is a crucial step to mastery of any endeavor, Jim never got the recognition he craved (this was part of his script). Susan's mother, Elaine, was a passive woman who thought it was her job to take care of her husband's fragile ego (her script), and she passed this coddling behavior on to her daughter. To distract herself from the anger she felt about her husband's constant need for attention, Elaine stayed up late at night to read and work on hobbies.

"When I was a girl, I just wanted Jim to be happy," Susan wrote. "His frustration explains why I felt so depressed around him. I feel the same way when I'm around men like him today. I can't concentrate on my needs, it's as though I fall under a spell."

Susan is describing the confusion that comes from identifying with her father's pain. Jim believed he was a victim of circumstances beyond his control, a dramatization Susan accepted as true when she was a girl because the alternative was unacceptable: Jim's immaturity was the cause of his failures. She repeated this script when she married, and subsequently she divorced two men who had unrealistic expectations. After the marriages were over, Susan fell into a depression, replaying the disappointment she felt when Jim let her down (disappointment is the script, the outcome Susan expects).

At another level, the men in Susan's life reflected her own spiritual malaise. Acknowledging that she believed life was an exercise in futility felt like suicide to Susan's ego, which had to be right ("It's them, not me!"). But admitting the truth ended her attraction to depressed men, although this did not happen overnight.

In one sense the men in Susan's life were secret allies, since their failures forced her to grow up and take responsibility. Had she married a capable man, she might have been tempted to live through him. On the other hand, his example could have inspired her. But when Susan took the risks that scared her, this transformed her character from Victim to Victor.

Transformation of character is the theme of every great story, the reason why readers keep turning the pages. In Hawthorne's classic tale *The Scarlet Letter*, for example, the heroine, Hester, begins the journey to self-awareness when she is thrown out of her village for committing adultery with the town's weak young minister, whom Hawthorne aptly named Dimmesdale.[7]

After Hester has nothing more to lose, she sees the villagers' hypocrisy and her lover's cowardice. She also becomes conscious of formerly hidden thoughts and feelings. Rather than leave, Hester settles down in a cottage outside the village to bring up her illegitimate daughter, Pearl, while earning her living as a seamstress. Banishment from the village forces Hester to overcome her fear that she cannot survive on her own. She not only survives; she grows into a wise, independent woman. The people in the village who judge Hester so harshly remain in perpetual childhood because they want to belong to the group more than they want to be individuals. Ironically, Hawthorne's message throughout his story is that the group is always wrong; it's only the individual (Hester) who sees the truth. But this doesn't happen until Hester is outside the group. Alone and abandoned, she finds her *self*, the happy ending to the story.

Times have changed since Hawthorne wrote his masterpiece about courage in the face of group condemnation. Yet fear of what the group thinks is still a common fear, with good reason. In some parts of the world, you lose your life and the lives of those you love when you threaten the powers that be. On a more mundane level, the fear of losing what you have can shut down self-expression. But as Hester (and Susan) discovered, the soul's integrity is worth any price.

Finding the Authentic Self

As you work on your story, you will see a thread that runs through your experiences, the lesson you are here to learn (and learn and learn). You will also see when and why people blamed you for their mistakes, when and why you blamed others, and when you were honest in spite of the emotional and financial risks. And you will become aware of the sweeping societal changes that you experienced as your generation moved through the decades. In that sense, writing your life story resets your mental and emotional software to present time.

For example, you were born after the Second World War, a period when an adult-centered world at war changed into a child-centered family unit at peace. This was the era of returning GIs going back to work or to college, and a baby boom that sparked the proliferation of schools, tract homes, freeways, automobiles, and television. The postwar family model of prosperity and stability matched almost no one's experience, except on television shows. Nonetheless, the picture of perfection worked its way into the collective subconscious, which left many people feeling shortchanged when life failed to live up to their expectations, as you saw with Susan.

In contrast, the Depression generation just before your time grew up in an entirely different world. Instability and scarcity were the norm during a decade of cutbacks that forced people to make do with very little and to be grateful, by and large, for what they had. It also caused this generation to value security over change. Additionally, Depression-era babies were few and far between and not as important to their families as children became in subsequent generations. Children of Depression-era parents knew adults had survival, not them, on their minds.

Those born after 1946 who later became parents tended to give a great deal of time, money, and attention to their children. It's not surprising that children of parents born after 1946 thought life began with their births. You probably didn't know much about the generation that preceded your parents', since life revolved around you, parents, siblings, teachers and friends at school, and kids in the neighborhood. But whether you knew them or not, your grandparents were powerful influences on your life, as you have seen in previous stories. This is because of the impact they had on your parents' thinking. Unless both of your parents were able to separate truth from fiction, you took in your grandparents' erroneous beliefs along with your morning oatmeal.

As an example, futility is a common script in alcoholic families. This is because alcoholics set goals they can't reach, not only for themselves but also for those who live and work around them, which generates the sense of futility. (I discuss realistic goals in chapter 6.)

The good news is that you are not condemned to repeat the family script, since there is more to you than biology and family conditioning. You have a creative spirit that longs to be free to live the rest of your life to the fullest. But first you must want to be free, and you must be willing to do the work freedom requires.

More on the Drama Triangle

As discussed previously, the purpose of the roles in the Drama Triangle is to perpetuate the life script. Being a Victim, Rescuer, or Persecutor is a substitute for genuine relating, where communication is honest and direct, as opposed to dishonest and indirect. This was certainly true for Julie, whose "I'm selfish if I take care of my needs" script attracted people who expected her to put their needs first.

Think of the script as a third party, like the director of a movie in which you and the supporting actors play the roles assigned to you. If you sign up for the Victim role ("poor me"), you can't solve problems, so you expect people to solve them for you. As a Rescuer ("let me help you"), you are supposed to solve others' problems, and when you don't you feel guilty. When your role is Persecutor ("it's all your fault"), others are responsible for your problems, so you are mad all the time. Can you see how these three scripts interconnect and that the outcome in every case is failure?

The next time you read a novel; watch a movie, video, or television drama; or listen to the lyrics of a "he/she done me wrong" song, notice who plays the roles in the Drama Triangle. The conversation goes from "poor me" to "let me help you" to "it's all their/your fault," and then it starts all over again.

To opt out of the roles in the Drama Triangle, you need to become aware of the roles you play. This is not easy, since script behavior is automatic: stimulus then response, stimulus then response. For example, someone you know has a habit of making poor choices and is about to make another mistake. *Without thinking* you offer a solution. The game begins. The other person appears to change, so you feel hopeful (the hook). Then he (or she) does what he has always done and fails. Now you feel hopeless. The game ratchets up a notch.

When you say anything about the poor choice, the other person makes excuses, rationalizes with, "Well, I'm getting better," or the conversation shifts to what you do wrong (gotcha). Then you question yourself, feel guilty, or get angry, all of which ups the ante. Then the other person gets defensive, and the game escalates until the relationship stalemates or ends: game, set, and match (remember the goal for both of you is failure, not success). Does this sound familiar?

To keep the game going, first you have to blind yourself to the other person's part of the problem. Then you have to continue in this denial so as not to threaten the relationship. To change, you have to be willing to try what feels uncomfortable and wrong. For instance, someone you know complains about an ongoing problem and then asks you what to do. This time you say (and mean it), "What do you think will solve the problem?" If this person asks what you think, you say what you think and leave it at that. Don't check back to see how she is doing.

When you catch yourself playing the role of the Victim, focus on the solution to the problem instead of complaining or hoping someone will rescue you. When you are tempted to play Rescuer, let the other person work through the difficulty — or not work through it. Nurture and encourage, but don't enable. Instead, trust that people can solve their problems if they are willing to do the work. As the poet Keats said when he heard about the misfortune of a friend, "He will have the pleasure of trying the resources of his spirit."[8]

When anger or impatience causes you to shift to the role of Persecutor, accept responsibility for your part of the problem. If you are involved with people who play any of the roles in the Drama Triangle, say to yourself, "This is a game that always ends in failure, and I choose not to play." This decision puts you in the role of the Victor, the person who solves problems.[9]

Deciding

You may have noticed that I use the word *decide* frequently. You might think only positive choices are decisions, and that negative outcomes happen to you. As a child you were not always conscious that you were making decisions, but you were making them nonetheless. Of course, some things are beyond your control — genetics, natural disasters, taxes, and death — but as an adult you always have control over how you react to what happens. No one can make you feel or think anything.

If you look in your dictionary for the word *decide*, you'll find that one definition is to bring something to an end. As you know, you do not end anything because of pressure from others. You may stop what you're doing for a time, but when the pressure is off you go back to your old ways.

Change takes place when you choose freely, consciously, and willingly. Until then you fake it, or you arrange to let someone else make the choice for you. Or someone sets you up to choose by using guilt or threats. Then whatever you choose, it is his fault (he made me do it). Now everybody feels powerless.

Think about a habit you used to have, such as smoking or drinking or eating too much. Did people pressure you to quit? That didn't work, did it? In fact, you probably got mad at them for trying to control you, and to prove how independent you were you smoked or drank or ate even more (they can't tell me what to do). Until you decided to stop smoking, or drinking or eating too much, you kept on doing it, right? Maybe not as much, or you did it only sporadically, but your choice to continue did not end until you threw the mental switch once and for all. You followed the same procedure when you decided to work smarter, not harder, and to stand up to bullies rather than avoid them. Then you felt powerful.

Julie resolved a lifelong problem when she decided to draw good boundaries. Why would that be so difficult? Because allowing others to take advantage of her was less painful than feeling guilty about being selfish. Illogical, but there you are. Fortunately, Julie was willing to do whatever it took to end an exhausting role she'd accepted in the past.

Tolerating the void was a huge challenge for Julie. Without the distraction of others' problems, she was face-to-face with her own problems. Some days she doubted her sanity. Dizzy spells and feeling disoriented were just a few of the signs that her mental furniture was being rearranged. This is an example of the discomfort that accompanies the middle stage of change, the Gobi Desert crossing that seems like an endless journey.

Julie still feels anxious when she takes certain risks, but she accepts discomfort as a sign that she's making healthy choices, not that she is wrong or selfish. Today, she has cordial, albeit distant relationships with some family members. She is close to those who are open to change and growth.

The Missing-Father Script

Societal scripts, like individual scripts, are based on illogical thinking. Just as you can jump to wrong conclusions under pressure, leaders in society make hasty decisions during times of social, political, and economic upheaval. Later, politicians and their constituents have to face the consequences of this bad judgment. Whenever I ask clients about the poor choices they made in the past, invariably they say, "I wasn't thinking clearly."

An example of not thinking clearly is the societal script "Father knows best." We all hope there is a father figure somewhere who has all the answers (Rescuer). Then we will not have to do the painful work of thinking for ourselves (Victim). While some fathers know what they are doing, no one knows what is best for everyone, as dictators (Persecutors) prove to their oppressed subjects.

I focus on the father in my work because the word *father* is a symbol for authority, the step-by-step process that leads to mastery. If your father did not master the work he loved, you have to look elsewhere for examples of success. This is why how-to books are so popular: they fill the father gap that opened wide following the Great Depression.

The missing-father syndrome so prevalent today is a metaphor for the lack of self-discipline. Just as members of a society that is out of control need to exercise self-restraint, those who search for a father substitute need to develop the inner strength that will guide them to success. Think of discipline as the friend you can depend on when life gets hard. Whatever you suffered and endured, saw and heard, felt and desired — every act of meanness and kindness you experienced — discipline was there to bring you through the experience.

Discipline solves a problem by turning you into a more effective person, as when you decide to save part of your income and invest it rather than spend everything you earn. Or you forgo quick and easy solutions for what works in the long-term. Discipline strengthens your personality through delays, setbacks, and restrictions.

In fairy tales, discipline is portrayed as the prince who searches for his lost princess. He finds his true love, but only after passing difficult tests. At the end of his arduous journey, the prince embraces the princess and they live happily ever after. Happily-ever-after stories are eternally relevant because they describe the journey to individuation, Jung's term for the process of becoming a whole, integrated individual. The beasts, dragons, and witches symbolize the parts of the personality we need to accept as our own if we are to become mature. Rejecting or projecting these traits keeps us in a childish stage of development.

For example, *Sleeping Beauty* is about a girl (the authentic self) who is cursed by the power of the evil witch (the fear of criticism) around the age of puberty (the birth of the script). She sleeps in her glass coffin until the prince (the rational mind) hacks his way through the weeds and brambles (fear and self-doubt) that surround Beauty's castle. When the prince finds the princess, he awakens her with the kiss of true love (self-acceptance). Then they live happily ever after, the personality united, as opposed to split into warring factions (I discuss the authentic self further in chapter 5).

Like the prince, you must pass through the forest of fear and self-doubt to reach your authentic self; the autobiography you write will guide you. After reading the previous chapter, you eliminated everything except what you use and love. In this chapter you get rid of everything except the real you. You may think you don't remember anything about the past or that your story is too boring to write about. But once you put pen to paper, or fingers to the keyboard, memories will come charging out of the subconscious like kindergartners at recess.

In case you think the stories I read are only about people who always succeed, let me assure you that my clients' autobiographies (and mine) are full of mistakes and poor judgment. When they send me stories that sugarcoat the past, I say, "Okay, now that you've given me the Disneyland interpretation, let me have the Anaheim version." After we both laugh, these clients say they didn't want to tell me what really happened for fear that I wouldn't want to work with them (the fear of criticism). There you have the *Leave It to Beaver* view of life I discussed at the beginning of this chapter: if you are struggling, there must be something wrong with you. But in fact the opposite is true: if you are struggling, you're probably doing everything right, since struggle is a sign that you're growing. By *struggle* I don't mean being a long-suffering martyr. I'm referring to the effort it takes to peel away the layers of lies and self-deception that surround the real you. *Then* life gets easy.

If you don't believe me, look around you. The land of inertia is packed with inhabitants at all hours of the day and night. They do everything except be honest with themselves, and then they wonder why they fail. How startled my clients are when I say struggle makes a character interesting; characters who don't struggle are boring because they never change.

At some level, we would all prefer to live in a Garden of Eden, where food drops from the trees and an omniscient God takes care of everything. But the truth is (and my view is that God knows this), we are never happy until we do what is difficult for us. What is difficult for you may not be difficult for me or anyone else. Only you know what you need to do to feel good about yourself. So don't hide from or shade the truth because of a fear of criticism. If you do, you will sabotage the exercise. Instead, take on the project as your contribution to society. Clearing your mental closet will make the world a more orderly place. You will also leave your children and grandchildren with only their own psychological closets to clean.

No one is going to read what you write unless you choose to show your work, so let it all out. At first what you write will seem gloomy and pessimistic, like the last act of *Othello*, when dead bodies litter the stage floor. Or you may think that you are being disloyal to the family, that you are being too hard on everyone, or that you are not seeing things accurately. Writing about some events will make you so depressed you won't want to get out of bed in the morning. When you realize how badly you were treated, you will feel very angry. Some of your choices will make you wonder how you could have been so stupid. Not to worry. All these reactions mean the excavation process is working. By the time you finish the story, you will have a novelist's point of view, meaning that you will see all your choices as necessary for character development.

Remember that character development is the hallmark of a good story. What matters is what the character does *after* poor choices. Does the hero or heroine make wiser choices? As John Milton said in his treatise on free choice (*Areopagitica*, written in 1644): "That which purifies us is trial, and trial is by what is contrary." To be virtuous we have to succumb to temptation, wrestle with the choice, and then reject it, Milton said.[10] This means that goodness is the result of trying the alternative, not avoiding that choice in order to look good. After all, what would Hester have become had she not fallen in love with the cowardly minister? Who would Susan be without the depressed men in her life? Who would you be without your poor choices?

Don't forget to refer to your grandparents and parents by first names *all the way through the story*. If you have trouble doing this, it means you're holding on to a child's idealized and highly charged view of the family. You may think you won't be able to live without these illusions. On the contrary, you are *not* living because of them!

Here is a motto you can write on a Post-it and stick on your computer: "Reality is my best friend; illusion is my worst enemy."

Your Grandparents' Scripts

To understand a character in a story, you have to watch what she does over time. As the story progresses, choices become consistent. Soon, you can predict what the character will do. Based on what you remember about your grandparents, what was predictable about their choices?

Who played the role of Victim (poor me), Rescuer (let me help you), or Persecutor (it's all your fault)? Did they change these scripts? If so, who was the Victor who solved problems? Who was honest and direct, as opposed to dishonest and indirect?

Describe your grandparents' experiences with money and work. Were they stingy or generous? Did they like their work, or was work survival? If you don't know the answers to these questions, ask your parents. If they are not alive or available, extrapolate from your parents' experiences with money and work or your own experiences with money and work.

Note the repetitive family experiences in the following excerpt from one of my client's autobiographies. I have changed his name and some of his circumstances to protect his privacy, as I have done with all the stories in the book.

Mike was a high-earning salesman in his midfifties. His story was a series of battles with authority figures who always let him down. He would get just so far in his career, and then he would sabotage success by procrastinating (ah, I see you know where this is going). Here is what Mike wrote about his paternal grandfather. My comments are in parentheses: "My grandfather was an immigrant. He was a hard worker, but he didn't think things through. He went bankrupt in a business he owned with his mother. This was devastating to her." (Why did the mother get into business with a son who didn't think things through? You know the answer — she was a Rescuer.)

"Money was always scarce, but he and my grandmother eventually paid all the money back to their creditors," Mike wrote. "He worked in several jobs, while she managed a factory during World War II. She worked into her seventies and lived to be ninety-nine. She clearly ran things." (Again, the woman thinks things through.)

"Love was — well, based on what I knew about my grandfather, he was the stern, silent type who believed children should be seen and not heard. They were put to bed right after their dinner so that he and my grandmother had time to themselves," Mike noted. (Mike said he thought the unusually early bedtime for the children was because his grandfather wanted all of his wife's attention.)

"My maternal grandmother was a strong woman too. After her husband died, she ran a grocery store that did very well, which was unusual for the Great Depression. Then she married a man who earned a good wage for the time. He was a soft touch.

"My mother was very indulged by her father when she was growing up," Mike wrote. "She never lacked for anything." (Indulgence fosters dependence.)

Based on what Mike wrote, what roles in Dr. Karpman's Drama Triangle did the grandfather play? Can you guess what roles the grandmother played? What roles do you think their sons and daughters played? What role would Mike play?

Of course, it's unfair to expect people to display consciousness that was not there in past generations. This would be rather like expecting people to get over serious infections before penicillin was invented. No one was in therapy except rich people, and there were no how-to books on the market to help people understand the family. Today, understanding the family is a mainstream endeavor; witness the therapy industry and the copious amount of books on how-to shelves in book-stores.

The more he understood his grandfather, the more Mike understood his father, a salesman who told Mike he drank because drinking was expected in business (it's all their fault). Mike said his father and mother played all three roles in the Drama Triangle, especially when they got drunk. The parents' stormy relationship put Mike and his siblings into various roles in the Drama Triangle. Mike repeated this script at home and at work, until he went into therapy after a second divorce (his third marriage works!).

The last hurdle was Mike's work. His current boss, the owner of the company, promised more than he could deliver because he wanted to make a big splash in his industry, and then blamed Mike for not making his numbers (see the Drama Triangle here?).

By the time Mike got to the end of his story, he realized he had consistently ignored his feelings when he made choices, and had then become angry about the consequences (Victim/Persecutor). "I kept going to work for men who didn't think things through, but that was true of me. I knew what was going on when I made those choices, but I didn't take the time to listen to myself," Mike said to me, opting out of the Drama Triangle.

"Well, now you will," I said, smiling.

When I asked Mike what kind of work he would do even if he did not get paid for it (I discuss this idea in chapter 4), he said he would like to work for himself and write a book. Just voicing the need for independence and creativity took Mike out of the role of Victim. To test his idea, he talked with managers and owners whose companies were in varying stages of sales development (I cover this process in chapter 7). Then he spoke with colleagues and salespeople he had mentored in the past. Mike's meetings confirmed that he was fascinated (passion clue) by the start-up phase of any endeavor. Once things were up and running, he was ready to move on to the next challenge. Repositioning himself as a sales troubleshooter, he also defined the market for the book he wanted to write. "I'll target the non-sales executive who needs to know what I know," Mike said. "Experienced salespeople will enjoy the book too."

Mike's story took a surprising turn, which I describe in chapter 7. It's proof that finding passion is a process.

Now let's go back to your grandparents' stories. How did they bring up your parents? Were they indulgent or firm, consistent or inconsistent? Were children to be seen and not heard? Or were children treated with respect and courtesy? (Be sure to use first names when recording your answers.)

What role did religion play in the formation of your grandparents' scripts? Did their beliefs stress obedience to authority? Or was life about becoming true to oneself? What was the effect of your grandparents' beliefs on your parents? Did they question what they were taught? Or did they copy their parents' beliefs?

What did (and do) you admire about your grandparents? What made you feel uncomfortable? Which grandparents adapted to the times? Who always did everything the same way (my way or the highway)? How their lives turned out will answer these questions for you.

Your Parents' Scripts

Again, think of your parents (use their first names) as characters in a story, not as relatives. This may be hard at first, but if you try you will eventually think of them as separate from you and of yourself as separate from them (even when they still see you as an extension of themselves).

Start your parents' stories with a description of how they met, since that meeting sets the tone for the relationship. Who introduced them? How old were they? How long did they know each other before they were a couple? Why did your parents continue to spend time together? If you don't know the answers to these questions, and if your parents are still alive, ask them.

Were your father's and mother's (first names) expectations realistic or unrealistic? When needs were not met, how did they cope with frustration? When they had conflicts, how did they resolve their differences, or were they never resolved? Were your parents more authentic as they aged, or did their ideas and attitudes stay the same?

How would you describe your parents' experiences with money, work, and relationships? What roles in the Drama Triangle did they play: Victim, Rescuer, or Persecutor? If they stopped playing these roles, what or who caused them to change?

If your parents divorced, who initiated the separation and what was the cause? Describe how each parent handled the aftermath of divorce and how that affected you. Did they remarry? If so, to whom? Was this relationship a repeat of their scripts, or was it a new experience?

Was your father (first name) a responsible parent? Did he succeed in the work he loved? Was he open or resistant to correction? In what way is he different now from the person he was when you were young? If he were not your father, would you want to spend time with him? Would he want to spend time with you if you were not related to him?

Was your mother (first name) a responsible parent? If she worked outside the home, did she succeed in the work she loved? Was she open or resistant to correction? In what way is she different now from the person she was when you were young? If she were not your mother, would you want to spend time with her? Would she want to spend time with you if you were not related to her?

Describe the houses or apartments in which the family lived while you were growing up. Were your homes orderly or chaotic, up-to-date or outdated? What did the homes say about your parents? Did the homes reflect who they were?

If your parents are still alive, what are their circumstances? Do they have good boundaries? What did (and do) you admire about each of them? Have you told them how you feel? What do they do that makes you feel angry or uncomfortable? Have you told them how you feel about this? If not, what would you say?

If your parents are deceased, were they happy with the way their lives turned out? Or did their stories end tragically (here, *tragedy* is defined as the consequences of our poor choices, not what others do to us).

Your Script

As you can see, being born is like starting a book in the next-to-last chapter. To understand the author's intent, you have to go back and read from the beginning. By now you know that your script began before you were born, and changing it takes insight and determination. After all, you are not just trying to change your script and your family's scripts; you are changing societal scripts about money, work, and relationships as well — no easy task.

When you feel overwhelmed, take a break from writing so you can sort through what's going on inside you, since that's probably what you did not do at the time the event took place. Pay attention to your dreams during this time, since often they reveal answers to questions that come up during the writing process.

One client could not understand why she felt so depressed as she wrote about her divorce; she thought she had gotten over the loss. Then Janet dreamt she attended a farewell party for her former spouse and that she left early. As she thought about her dream, it occurred to Janet that she had said good-bye to her husband (she went to the party), but she had cut off the grieving process (she left early).

Her subconscious came to Janet's aid with the step she needed to finish, accepting the finality of the loss. Completing the last stage of grief brought her into present time. Then she was free to form a new attachment.

Describe any traumatic losses that took place in your family. Were these losses acknowledged and grieved? Was emotion freely expressed? Or did family members freeze grief in the shock stage, as was true in Maria's family?

"It was like living in an icehouse," Maria said about her parents' house after her older brother's accidental death. The appearance of life went on, but *life* stopped when the mother's favorite son died. She wouldn't allow anyone to discuss the death; instead she changed the subject when someone tried to do so. Not surprisingly, Maria concluded that painful feelings must be so bad they had to be avoided at all costs. From then on, when feelings of sadness, anxiety, and depression arose, Maria numbed them with food and excessive socializing.

To change her illogical "painful feelings are bad" script, Maria needed to see the value in pain, that pain is one way she would know she was alive. In time and with practice, Maria was able to feel sadness and anxiety without distraction.

"Everything makes sense now," Maria said when we met to talk about that section of her story. "My mother was afraid the pain would never end, so she wouldn't take the first step, nor would she ask for help. How very sad," Maria sighed. "My brother would not have wanted her to do that to herself, or to us. He would have said, 'Grieve the loss, and then go on with your life, Mom, and let others talk about how they feel.' That's the kind of guy he was: wise for his years."

Thinking about what her brother would have said helped Maria to be more objective. "I felt angry with my mother for not letting us express our feelings, and that was a necessary step. But now that I feel painful emotions, I understand and forgive her for not wanting to deal with them. Grief is hard work. In the future, when people can't handle my pain I'll do what my brother would advise, 'Let it be, Maria.'"

Accepting what you can't change is grief's greatest gift, according to David Kessler, an expert on death and dying like his mentor, Elisabeth Kübler-Ross. He writes movingly on his website about the five stages of grief: denial, anger, bargaining, depression, and acceptance. Kessler says the *denial* stage prepares the mind for loss. It's how the brain copes when feeling overwhelmed. We can take in only so much. The next stage of grief is *anger*. Anger is like a bridge that connects us to the person or object we lost. As long as we're angry, we don't feel the emptiness. Then we move into the third stage of grief: *bargaining*. We think about what might have been, "if only," and "what if." As the loss sinks in, we experience sadness and *depression*, the fourth stage of grief. After we work through depression, we are ready for the final stage of grief, *acceptance*. Acceptance does not imply that we are okay with the loss, Kessler says. It means we have learned to accept and live with the loss.[11]

Now let's go back to your story. Describe what was going on in the family before you were born. As an example, were you the latest arrival in a large family? If so, were you a welcome newcomer, or were you one more mouth to feed? If you were an only child, how did your birth change your parents' lives?

Even the most devoted parents have days when they feel ambivalent about the demands of parenthood. This doesn't mean they don't love their children; it means they are human. As a child or adolescent, however, you may have interpreted occasional parental ambivalence as your being unwanted or unloved. For the young, love is all or nothing, and this intensity is both wonderful and exhausting. That you can love someone and not want to have that person around all the time is beyond the immature psyche.

As you think about your parents as human beings, you may realize they loved you more than you knew. You were too wrapped up in yourself to notice how much they sacrificed for your well-being, such as working two jobs to make sure you had clothes, food to eat, and a roof over your head. Or you may realize that the people who were your parents did not love. Instead, they expected (and may still expect) you to love them, which is why you felt unloved in their presence.

It takes time and a great deal of objectivity to see that what parents do is not personal. It's just what they do, given their level of consciousness. There is no excuse for abuse, but many parents repeat what was done to them, until they become conscious enough to feel remorse for the pain they cause others and themselves.

Temperament

How you derive energy indicates your temperament. If you are ener-
gized around people, you are an extrovert. If you recharge when you are
alone, you are an introvert. If you were an introverted child, did anyone know you needed to be alone to recharge? Or did you hear, "Why
don't you go out and play with the other children?" when you were
happily reading a book? Was this when you decided there must be
something wrong with you? (Remember, you are looking for the illogical decisions you made that only you can change.)

If you still feel guilty about not wanting to be around people, it
helps to think of the advantages you have as an introvert: the ability to
concentrate, to tackle long projects, and to get to the bottom of any
problem. According to experts on temperament, the capacity to delve
deeply puts you in the creative minority of the population.[12]

If you were an extroverted child, you may have felt guilty for wanting to be around other people, especially if one or both of your parents
were introverts. Did you get the social interaction you needed? Did
your parents know that you got depressed when you were alone too
long? Were you allowed to be who you were, or were you criticized a
great deal?

Adults who are not aware of differences in temperament can do a
great deal of damage to children. For example, extroverted parents and
teachers may push introverted children to talk and socialize too much.
Then they may blame the children for being overstimulated or chron-
ically ill. To please extroverted adults, these children try to be like them
and then get exhausted and depressed.

Extroverted children suffer from the lack of stimulation when they
are forced to be alone too long. They learn to feel badly about themselves when introverted parents and teachers criticize them for needing
to talk and socialize. Losing touch with the authentic self is the sad result for both extroverts and introverts. The best way to get over past
misunderstandings is to accept that your temperament is different, not

better or worse, and to see the advantages you have as an introvert or an extrovert. As you will see in chapter 7, your temperament is part of what defines your perfect niche.

School Years

Think about how you handled the transition from staying home to being in school most of the day. Were you frightened and overwhelmed by the noise, teasing, snobbery, and bullying that takes place in schools? Or did you hold your own in the group situation?

What was your strategy of coping with new situations: observe and then jump in, or did you jump in and then observe? Is this how you cope with new situations today? Do you size up the situation before acting? Or do you leap in with guns blazing? Which choice describes intelligent behavior?

The late John Holt was an innovative thinker on the subjects of learning and intelligence. Two of his books sold millions of copies, and they are still on the must-read lists of many teachers and parents: *How Children Fail* and *How Children Learn*.[13] Holt describes intelligence as

a way of behaving in various situations, and particularly in new, strange, and perplexing situations. The true test of intelligence is not how much we know how to do, but how we behave when we don't know what to do.

The intelligent person, young or old, meeting a new situation or problem, opens himself [or herself] up to it; he tries to take in with mind and senses everything he can about it; he thinks about *it*, instead of about himself or what it [the situation] might cause to happen to him; he grapples with it boldly, imaginatively, resourcefully, and if not confidently at least hopefully; if he fails to master it, he looks without shame or fear at his mistakes and learns from them. This is intelligence. Clearly its roots lie in a certain feeling about life, and one's self with respect to life. Just as clearly, unintelligence is not what most psychologists seem to suppose, the same thing as intelligence only less of it. It is an entirely different style of behavior, arising out of an entirely different set of attitudes.[14]

Later in life, Holt decided that, because of institutional resistance to change, it wasn't possible to reform elementary education, so he encouraged parents to take charge. His suggestions on how to educate children at home pioneered the home-schooling movement.

I include Holt's comments made during an interview with *Mother Earth News*, since they may indicate when and why you decided *not* to trust your authentic self:

> It is a well-established principle that if you take somebody who is doing something for her or his own pleasure and offer some kind of outside reward for doing it — *and* let the person become accustomed to performing the task *for* that reward — then take the reward away, the individual will stop that activity. You can even train nursery school youngsters who love to draw pictures to *stop* drawing them, simply by giving them gold stars or some other little bonus for a couple of months... and then removing that artificial "motivation."
>
> In fact, I think that our society *expects* schools to get students to the point where they do things *only* for outside rewards. People who perform tasks for *their* internal reasons are hard to control. Now, I do not think that teachers get up in the morning and say to themselves, "I am going to go to school today and take away all those young people's internal motivations"... but that is exactly what often happens.[15]

As Holt states, children who do tasks for internal reasons are hard to control. They do what they want to do without checking in with peers or authority figures. By implication, externally motivated children are easier to control. For example, think about a time when you did what you wanted to do. Was it harder for people to influence you? Then recall a time when you worked for approval. Was it easier for people to influence you?

When you showed your work to parents, did they say, "Oh, that is really good," or did they express disapproval? After that, did you remember this reaction as you worked? Imagine how you would have felt if they had asked you to tell them about the work and what you were trying to accomplish? In other words, what if you had been taught to focus on what *you* thought and felt?

As an example of trusting yourself, what did you do when others disagreed with what you knew was right? Did you feel anxious and doubtful? Did you go to others for validation? Or did you hang in there with the anxiety until time proved you were right? Is this how you handle doubt today?

How did you cope with frustration when you were young? Did you complain or get sick hoping that would get you what you wanted? Or did you accept that you could not always have what you wanted when you wanted it? Is this how you deal with frustration now?

Describe how television affected your life. Did you compare your life to what you saw on the small screen? Did you believe television shows were true, or did you know that problems take longer than a half hour to solve?

What were your favorite books and magazines? How did these publications influence you? Which movies had a lasting effect on you? How did authors and scriptwriters influence your view of life in general?

Make a list of popular icons that influenced you: artists, musicians, and movie and television stars. How did an era of drugs, sex, rock and roll, and dropping out affect your attitude toward life? If you were not that affected by these influences, why was that the case?

Next, describe what your family thought was funny. Was family humor a mask for anger? When you protested against sarcastic or hurtful remarks, did you hear, "You're too sensitive" or "I was just kidding"? How would you describe your sense of humor: dry, witty, or boisterous? What or who makes you laugh? If you make others laugh, why is this so?

Did you live in just one or a few towns while growing up? Or did you move around a great deal? How did this affect your reaction to change? Describe how you react to change now: with excitement, dread, or fear?

Your authentic self was with you all during these years, storing information for you to sort through later, as you are doing now. You knew what was going on, although you may not have known how to express your thoughts and feelings about what you observed. Now is your chance.

Begin by introducing yourself (in an imagined dialogue) to your teenaged self. Say, "Hello, I'm the grown-up you. Guess what, we made it!"

Now ask the teenaged you what is going on in the family, what each parent needs to do to succeed. Next, ask what is going on at school and with friends. Then ask what the teenager needs to do to succeed (meaning, reach your full potential). You will be surprised by how much you knew back then.

Sometimes your rational mind (the prince) can work through the autobiography on its own. Or you may want professional help. If you are already working with a coach or counselor, reading your story will give that person insight that normally takes months of talking to bring to the surface. For most of my clients, the interactive autobiography is the culmination of years of inner scrutiny.

Leaving Home

By the time you reached your late teens, your choices were consistent and therefore predictable. What was predictable about the choices you made after high school? Which of these choices worked? Which choices always ended in failure?

What was going on when you left the family home for good? Were you pushed out, or did you leave on your own? How did you adjust to the freedom that came with being on your own? Did you like making your own decisions?

If you went to college, did you select the institution, was it your parents' choice, or was it a mutual choice? How did that choice work out for you? What did you gain from the experience, aside from academic knowledge? If you joined the military, traveled, went to work, or got married at an early age, describe the outcome of these choices, keeping the script in mind.

Describe how you got along with authority figures, including your parents. When did you begin to relate to them as an adult? Was this when you stopped looking to them for approval or money? Did independence take you and them out of the Drama Triangle? How did the way you related to your parents affect the way you related to other authority figures: bosses, experts, law enforcement officers, or government officials?

The word *authority* refers to people who know what they're doing, not just to people who are in a position of authority. Competent authorities got where they are because of their solid ability to lead. They are self-correcting, and they are open to correction. Is there anyone in your past or current life who fits this description of authority?

Some people are in such a hurry to get in positions of power that they skip the steps that prepare them for leadership, such as patience, self-discipline, and developing a positive attitude. They don't self-correct, nor do they accept correction. The longer they are in power, the more damage they do. How did you react to incompetent authority figures? Did you try to topple them from power, wait it out, smolder in silence, or leave? What do you do now around people who aren't up to the job?

If you were (and are) in a position of authority, what did you go through to prepare for the responsibility? Now that you're in a position of power, do you self-correct? Are you open to correction? Can you admit mistakes and apologize? Is this because you love what you're doing, and you care about the people who put their trust in you?

One of the more responsible choices you can make, aside from having children and letting them take risks (the biggest risk of all), is to start your own business. How old were you when you started your first venture? Have you always looked for ways to innovate or improve? (Again, you are looking for consistency of choices.)

Did you succeed in your business? If so, why? If you failed, what caused the failure? Did you try again until you got it right? If you are in business or you have your own practice or project to work on now, what do you need to change to make it work at this stage of life? (I discuss this in chapter 7.)

If you married or lived with others, did these relationships confirm your script, the outcome you expected? For example, were you consistently disappointed, mistreated, ignored, or frustrated? How would your former partners describe you? How did you fit their scripts?

The best relationships are mutual makeovers, meaning that each person is changed by the encounter. This can be a cooperative enterprise, a knock-down, drag-out fight, or both, depending on each party's resistance to change. Which relationships forced you to change and grow? What is better about you as a result of spending time with these people?

If you divorced or ended partnerships, what was the cause of the breakup? Did you initiate the ending, or did you let your partner end the relationship? What would you do now if you could go back in time? Have you accepted the finality of these losses and moved on?

If you are married or in a committed partnership, describe how this situation differs from previous choices. If you're alone, is this your choice, or are you afraid commitment will cause you to lose your freedom? What would give you the confidence that you can be in a committed relationship and maintain good boundaries?

Now, if you have children, write about them. Do you see them as separate from you, or do you think of them as your children? Do you and they have the same values? If not, do you feel comfortable with not wanting to be around them? Do you give them the right to call or contact you when they wish, or do you pressure them to stay in touch with you?

If I were to ask, "How would each of your children describe you?" would they say you're a good role model, or would they say they don't want to be like you? If either answer is true about you, why did your children come to this conclusion? If you agree, why? If not, why not?

Are you pleased with the way your children's lives have turned out so far? Do you feel responsible for the consequences of their choices? Or do you accept that they are responsible for their choices?

Do any of your children (and grandchildren) have scripts? Are these based on your script or your spouse or partner's script? If your children's scripts include addiction, what stage of life are they avoiding? What would change the outcomes of their stories?

How do you feel about the stage of life you're in now? Are you surprised by its advantages? Do you deal with the challenges with humor and grace, or would you rather be back in an earlier stage of life?

In Conclusion

Now it's time to wrap up your story (at last). First, summarize your experiences with money, work, and relationships. Do you have enough money, or is there never enough? Is work the way you express your natural gifts, or is work what you do for money? Is love emotional, financial, or sexual barter, or is love a gift freely given and received?

In an imagined dialogue, ask the supporting actors in your story to step forward and take a bow, beginning with your grandparents and parents. Thank them for what they gave you, not just genetic and material legacies but also traits like faith and persistence.

Next, thank each of your siblings for the times you shared growing up, even if today you have little in common. Express your gratitude to children and grandchildren. Then, ask extended family members to take a bow. Let them know how they affected (and continue to affect) your life.

Now thank your spouse(s) and lovers. This is a time when you'll have to be unusually objective, so be sure to keep your sense of humor. Then pay special tribute to people who would not settle for less than your best effort: teachers, coaches, and bosses. If you think these people would like to hear from you, send a letter or email that expresses your gratitude.

Don't forget to thank (again, in an imagined dialogue) the people who taught you painful lessons, such as the importance of avoiding them in the future. If you injured others, including family members, and you have not already apologized and made amends, ask for forgiveness. If anyone, including family members, injured you, let them know how they hurt you. Then forgive them.

Now wait a minute, you say, some of these people don't deserve forgiveness, because what they did was reprehensible. They should apologize and ask *me* for forgiveness; that's only fair. If I forgive them, won't they think they got away with what they did? Won't they see me as a patsy, a pushover? Where's the justice in that?

Forgiveness does not mean that you approve of the people who hurt you or that they are off the hook for what they did. Nor does forgiveness mean you have to let these people back in your life. That depends on how they treat you in the future. My point is that holding on to anger and resentment keeps you stuck in the roles of the Victim and Persecutor, replaying a story that always ends in failure. Forgiveness, on the other hand, severs the ties that bind you to those who injured you, and their ties to you. Then you are free and they are free. Now you don't have to think about these people anymore. You can think about something else: finding your passion. Be assured, a Power greater than any of us will take care of the people who harmed you, and probably already has, although you may not know how swift and precise retribution can be. Or sometimes the wheels of justice grind slowly, but grind they do.

Finally, commend yourself for the determination it took to get to where you are today. Life set up many hurdles for you to jump. Some were so high you thought you would never get over them. Others were surprisingly easy. But now you know how to jump and when not to jump. Or as the following poem by Portia Nelson makes clear, good judgment is perseverance in disguise.

AUTOBIOGRAPHY IN FIVE SHORT CHAPTERS

I.

I walk down the street.
There is a deep hole in the sidewalk.
I fall in.
I am lost . . . I am helpless.
It is not my fault.
It takes forever to find a way out.

II.

I walk down the same street.
There is a deep hole in the sidewalk.
I pretend I do not see it.
I fall in again.
I can't believe I am in the same place.
But it is not my fault.
It still takes a long time to get out.

III.

I walk down the same street.
There is a deep hole in the sidewalk.
I see it is there.
I still fall in . . . it is a habit.
My eyes are open.
I know where I am.
It is my fault.
I get out immediately.

IV.

I walk down the same street.
There is a deep hole in the sidewalk.
I walk around it.

V.

I walk down another street.[16]

SUMMARY

1. When did you conclude that your life was not going to end well?
2. What family circumstances influenced this decision?
3. Who were the supporting actors in your script?
4. What roles in the Drama Triangle did all of you play?
5. Are you ready to "walk down another street"?

CHAPTER 4

Recognize the Passion Clues and Off-Track Signals

No ultimate truth is true unless we love it.
— JOHN MIDDLETON MURRY

So here you are, moving along the passion path. You eliminated (or are eliminating) the distractions from your life: habits, possessions, and outdated ways of interacting with others. Then you wrote your life story, beginning with your grandparents' and parents' stories, calling everyone by his or her first name. Now you have more objectivity about your forebearers and the times in which they lived. The more you become aware of who you are (and who you are not), the more united you feel, as opposed to feeling divided. To your relief, the healthy individual you are becoming is who you have always wanted to be.

Objectivity also revealed to you when you and others got caught in the roles in the Drama Triangle. Now, when you find yourself playing the roles of Victim, Rescuer, or Persecutor, you exit stage right. If you do fall back into these roles, you get out immediately without blaming others or yourself.

Now you're ready to take the next step into the unknown, recognizing the passion clues. And since you learn by observing what does not work, as well as what does work, you will also learn about the signals that let you know when you're off the passion path.

John Middleton Murry's comment under this chapter's heading implies that whatever you love is also true. Murry was for many years a renowned figure on the English literary scene. The quotation is from his book about John Keats, specifically his analysis of the meaning of Keats's famous line "Beauty is truth, and truth beauty." Murry interprets this concept as follows:

> Love alone will change fact into Truth. And this, however strange it may sound, is no foolish fancy. For Love is a faculty of understanding, and unless it enters into and transmutes our knowledge of fact, we cannot really know. It is not that the fact is changed by Love; but only by Love can it be fully seen. For the presence of Love in knowledge is the evidence that the total [man], and not merely the partial...man, responds to the total thing.[1]

For Keats, nothing was more important than the "holiness of the heart's affections." Although he was a deeply affectionate young man, he was referring not to sentimental attachment but to profound appreciation for "the light and the shade" of life. Equal acceptance of the light and the shade was certainly the theme in Keats's story. In spite of critics, money woes, illness, unconsummated love, and his awareness of his impending early death, Keats remained a channel for the creative energy that transformed him as he wrote, maintaining a detached state of mind he called negative capability, the capacity of "being in uncertainties, mysteries, doubts, without any irritable reaching after fact and reason."[2]

Or as Krishnamurti said in one of his lectures, when you know love, self is not. The moment the mind ceases its endless chatter, you experience the unknown, he says — and in that emptiness is love. "Surely when you are completely open, when on all levels you are in complete communication, completely integrated, then there is joy and you begin to create.... Creativeness is a sense of total self-forgetfulness, when there is no turmoil, when one is wholly unaware of the movement of thought."[3] Krishnamurti is talking about how the mind functions when you are completely connected with what you are doing: the mind is quiet, so it is open to signals that were formerly blocked by fear and self-doubt. A calm, clear mind is the seedbed for inspiration; it is what Keats called negative capability.

It may be hard to imagine a state of mind in which there is no despair (poor me), feeling responsible for others' happiness (let me help you), or blaming others for your failures (it's all their fault). But detachment is not only possible, it's also the only way to be at peace when others are in pain, according to Al-Anon, a worldwide organization that offers a recovery program for the families and friends of alcoholics. What follows is this group's definition of detached love:

> Detachment is a tool that helps families to help themselves. Letting go of the obsession with another's behavior frees individuals to live happier and more manageable lives, lives with dignity and rights: lives guided by a Power greater than ourselves.
>
> Detachment is neither kind nor unkind; nor does it imply evaluation of the person or situation from which you are detaching. Detachment is simply a way to look at people and situations realistically and objectively, making intelligent decisions possible.[4]

Since alcohol and its effect on the family are themes in many of my clients' stories (and in society at large), I always ask, "How much do you drink?" when we begin working together. If I don't bring up alcohol and other addictions, a client's process of finding his passion will bog down and I won't know why.

When you total up the amount of alcohol being consumed, "one or two glasses of wine a night" adds up to quarts of chemicals entering a person's body each month. Some studies show that drinking a glass of red wine a day can be good for the body, but daily intake of alcohol is harmful when people use it to numb painful emotions. The difference is *why* one drinks: for pleasure or escape?

My clients come to understand why they drink only after they take alcohol out of their systems for six months. Some tell me that they just needed to stop drinking for a while to clear their minds. Others say they see what they could not see before. "It was as though a fever broke,"

Carolyn, one of my clients, said to me three weeks after she stopped drinking two glasses of wine every night. "Even my vision improved. My husband stopped drinking too. We realized we were both using alcohol to avoid our marital problems.

"We went to marriage counseling a few times, but the therapist never asked about alcohol. I think that's why therapy didn't work for us. I'm glad you suggested we take a look at our drinking habits," Carolyn said. "Not only do we look and feel better but also our communication has improved. We're much better listeners. We have wine with meals occasionally, but not when we need to talk about what's bothering us."

Unless therapists are familiar with the effects of alcohol through personal experience and training, they underestimate the impact of excessive alcohol consumption on relationships. Therapy can go on for years with no results because feelings are not being felt, processed, and expressed honestly.

It's not that I am against drinking alcohol. It depends on how often you drink and how alcohol affects you. Does a different personality emerge when you drink? Are you more belligerent, more morose, less outgoing, or less shy and reclusive? Do you always feel tired and hung over the next day, even after a couple of drinks? Is alcohol always a factor wherever you go? Do you get high to numb painful feelings? If you answered yes to any of these questions, cut back or stop drinking altogether. You will feel and look better, and you will also learn new ways to cope with the challenges that come at midlife and beyond.

Freeing the Emotions

As noted, the level of addiction in our society indicates the lengths to which people will go to avoid painful feelings. In spite of all evidence to the contrary, the belief persists that addictive highs are terrific substitutes for the natural high of emotional maturity. When painful feelings are not acknowledged and felt, they remain in a youthful stage of development. The mind goes on chronologically, but feelings are left behind, ignored like unwanted stepchildren. When crises occur, as they do throughout life, these unprocessed, immature emotions erupt like lava from an exploding volcano. You may have heard the phrase "arrested development" used to describe emotions that are back in time, meaning that they are relative to what happened long ago, not now.

My point is that when the feelings have yet to mature, or if you reject the value of feelings, you can't find, much less do, what you love for a living, since passion is the most intense feeling of all. Passion, or devotion, elevates your experience of life, but this doesn't mean your work is easy. On the contrary, passion is so demanding that sometimes you want to leave. You're not always comfortable, and your intensity will bother some people, but by the time you come to the end of life you will have no regrets, because you held nothing back.

So here are the five clues that let you know you're in tune with the holiness of your heart's affections, when life and work fit like a well-tailored garment. Again, I use the word *you* rhetorically, as I do all throughout the book, so interpret what I say as personal only if it applies to you or those you know.

Passion Clue #1.
You Would Do the Work Even If You Did Not Get Paid for It

This is the most difficult clue for many people to comprehend, and yet it's the most important clue of all. You may believe (or you used to believe before reading this book) that you can't make money doing what you love, and that only fools would work for nothing. Defining work as what you would rather not do probably began with the Garden of Eden story, in which Adam and Eve were thrown out of paradise for eating the apple that gave them the knowledge of good and evil. From then on, they (and the rest of us) were condemned to earn a living by the sweat of their brows — no more lounging around in paradise.

Interpreting the story as an allegory for psychological growth, however, suggests that we all have to leave childhood (the garden) if we are to become self-reliant adults. Otherwise, we remain eternal boys and girls looking for a father figure to make life easier for us. But literal-minded folks emphasized the sin part of the story, thus the belief that work is punishment for being disobedient. Moreover, past downturns in the economy, depressions, recessions, and the aftermath of wars led entire generations to conclude that work is for survival, not satisfaction and personal growth.

As a test, stop and think about the word *work*. Does work conjure up indenture, what you are doomed to do to support yourself and your family? Can you imagine work being what you enjoy so much that you would do it for nothing, even though others would pay you?

Passion is not a hobby, although a hobby can turn into a passion if it's what you want to do for others. This was true for Ann (described in chapter 1). She had always kept a journal — that was how she stayed sane, she said. But she could not imagine getting paid to do the things she did anyway. Most people don't like to write, or if they do they don't write as clearly as Ann does. So companies were glad to advertise on her blog, since her strong voice attracted their prime customers.

Ann could not see writing as part of her destiny, because writing did not feel like work. When she redefined work as enjoyment, however, writing a blog about sales became what Ann did when she was not running her recruiting business (also fun).

Notice what you enjoy that others think is hard work. What do you never get tired of doing? Do you want to do this for others, not just sometimes but day after day? Even when you have plenty of money, would you keep on doing it? It may not have occurred to you that people will pay for what you do on your own (remember what John Holt said about internal motivation?). But they will gladly pay if the activity solves their problems. And lo and behold, these just happen to be the problems you love to solve. In fact, you don't think of what you do as solving a problem; it's what you do for fun. Does the concept of having fun change your definition of work?

Passion Clue #2. Mastery Is Your Goal

The desire to master what you do is another sign you're on the passion path. You want to get it right, whatever "it" is, so you practice and practice, correcting yourself as you go along. You're not satisfied with less than your best effort. The desire to get better is a clue that you're doing what interests you. This is the same way you feel when you're with someone whose company you enjoy. You aren't wishing you were with someone else. Your attention is on the person in front of you, not on checking out other options.

Ambivalence and mastery are opposites, since half a heart is worse than none; at least none is definite. Mastery thrives on certainty, whereas ambivalence avoids making a choice because of a mental conflict. Until the inner war is resolved, you keep one eye on the exit. The autobiography project discussed in chapter 3 was designed to help you become aware of the inner conflicts — such as the fear of losing control — that keep you from finding your passion. As you will see in the next chapter, the false self throws out all the stops if it senses you are ready to change. Then you face a kind of final exam: you're tested with your worst fear to see if you are serious about commitment. So don't think you just choose passion and that's the end of the story.

In fact, as soon as you commit to your passion, fear comes to the surface like an underwater monster, swamping the boundaries of your rational mind. This intense reaction is a sign the choice is *working*, not that you made the wrong choice. After all, you wouldn't have such a powerful reaction if you didn't care so much about the outcome. On the other hand, when you make safe choices (no chance of failure), fear lies dormant in your subconscious, as when you hang out with people who don't challenge you. This can lull you into thinking that you've made the right choice, since you're so comfortable.

Ah, but if growth is your psyche's goal, you won't get away with the easy glide through life. Something or someone will come along and jar you out of your complacency. Lucky you! Wake-up calls can come in many disguises: you lose your job, business, a marriage partner, or you have an accident. If you see the positive change that comes from such reversals, you won't have to wait for the universe to bash you over the head to get your attention.

Being open to criticism is another indication that you're on the mastery track. The best critics want you to succeed, so they will tell you what you don't want to hear. Constructive critics are also generous with praise and encouragement. They don't give up on you, because they know the best result takes time.

Destructive critics are not interested in your success. They don't offer praise or encouragement. These critics are quick to give up on you, because they have yet to reach their goals, so the likelihood of your success causes them to feel envious. Envy can fuel a malicious desire to destroy or undermine another with gossip or criticism or, in its milder form, by damning another with faint praise. Jealousy is not to be confused with envy, since jealousy is what you feel when you are afraid someone will take what you have: a position, friendship, spouse, or lover. Envy is what you feel when *you* want what others have. Unlike envy, rivalry and competition can be seen in a positive light, as with a fierce competitor or rival in love, business, or sports. Then "may the best man [or woman] win" prevails, as when athletes compete for a gold medal, and companies are rivals for the consumer's dollar.

Of course, darker emotions are complex and often mixed, and all of us have, at times, felt them all at once, but according to *Webster's New Collegiate Dictionary*, "in spite of their shared element of meaning, these words [jealousy or rivalry] are not close synonyms [with envy] and can rarely be interchanged without loss of precision or alteration of emphasis."[5]

But since mastery is your goal, even destructive critics are seen as useful, because they force you to examine your assumptions, to see flaws that kinder critics overlook, and to stand up for what you know is true. When destructive critics turn out to be mirrors of your worst fear, such as the belief that you don't have what it takes to succeed or that you don't deserve to be successful, taking back those projections is cause for rejoicing.

Passion Clue #3. You Are Transformed as You Do the Work

The work that engages your heart and soul is your one and only love: there is nothing else you want to do, nowhere else you want to be but where you are. Within the confines of commitment, you are forced to face and work through your fears and inadequacies, which changes you into a better person. As the years go by, love for what you do grinds away the layers of self-deception until all that's left is your authentic self. This is a brutal way to grow, but it's thorough. Spiritually speaking, the passionate get richer and richer and the uncommitted get poorer and poorer.

Passion can begin as a personal desire, something you want just for you. But the longer you do the work, the more you see that your goals are universal goals: everyone wants what you want. The way you express this collective longing transforms you into an instrument of change, which gives your life meaning and purpose.

Another sign that you're on the mastery track is that you sense a force opening certain doors for you and closing others forever. No matter how hard you push, these doors will not open. You have no choice but to surrender to a Power greater than your own.

Over the years, passion for your work separates you from all that is not true. The old self dies and the new, wiser, more tolerant self is reborn on the morrow. But what you keep forever is gratitude for the transformative power of love: "Love is patient and kind; love does not envy or boast; it is not arrogant or rude; does not insist on its own way; it is not irritable or resentful; does not rejoice in wrongdoings, but rejoices with the truth. Love bears all things, believes all things, hopes all things, and endures all things. Love never ends" (1 Corinthians 13:4–11). Like the beam from a lighthouse, love for your work is not diminished by the winds of adversity, nor does your commitment waver in the face of criticism or condemnation. Human approval may come and go, but the approval that lasts flows from a boundless source of energy. Those who work with love know God.

Passion Clue #4. You Are Not Aware That Time Is Going By

A sense of timelessness is another clue that you are on the passion path. Your mind is on what's in front of you, like a child on the beach with a bucket and shovel building a sand castle. You wake up in the morning and the next thing you know it's evening. Where did the time go, you ask yourself? Every day it is the same: there is no past or future, only now. But as soon as fear enters your mind, boundaries go up and you are in the past or the future, worrying about what you cannot control.

Anxiety about being out of control causes your mind to race back and forth as it tries to get in control, like a warrior running amok on the battlefield. You worry about not having enough money, being criticized, losing love, your health, getting old, and dying. If you can turn off this horror movie for a moment, the mind calms down, as when you wake up from a nightmare. Then you see that fear determines your experience of time. The less fear, the more you remain where there is no time.

Don't confuse a sense of timelessness with vagueness, being late, or "forgetting" appointments and responsibilities. Drifting along in a dreamy fog is not living in the moment; it's passive avoidance (you can't make *me* do what I don't want to do). Ah, the Drama Triangle.

Paradoxically, people who master the details of life are more likely to live in the moment. They don't worry about details; they just take care of them. As in a house that is always free of clutter, there is nothing in the background to distract them. They are right here, right now, paying close attention because they don't want to miss anything.

Passion clue number 4 lets you know you're out of the dungeon of fear and in the realm of the spirit. Then daily life is a microcosm of the eternal, an opportunity to learn. You are the satellite's camera that orbits high above the earth, seeing the near and far with equal clarity.

Passion Clue #5. You Are Paid to Be Who You Are

When you were growing up, you were taught that you were many things: your family, nationality, religion, race, and gender. Later, you were defined by what peers and authority figures thought of you.

As an adult, you find that your value is measured by the level of your education and training, your accomplishments, possessions, friends, and the person you live with or marry; even your children and grandchildren and what they achieve measure your value. But who are you without anything and anyone to define you? If you were in a strange country where you knew no one and no one knew you, who would you be then? When you get paid to be this person, your authentic self, you are definitely on the passion path.

If you're an introvert, you work in a quiet place with few interruptions, at your own pace, and in your own way. You have the right mixture of stimulation and solitude to keep you centered and balanced. Your partner and close friends share your love of contemplation. You are at your best when you research, write, think, and create. You are comfortable alone, one-on-one, and in small, intimate groups, but large groups tire you. You know your limits, and you don't go beyond them.

If you're an extrovert, you work and live in a stimulating environment. You're at your best when you travel to new and faraway places. You charge up in groups, meetings, and at conferences and parties. You love being in the limelight, either on stage or in front of a television camera or a microphone. Performing in front of an audience makes good use of the strengths that come naturally to you. You enjoy some time alone, but most of the time you like to be around people, talking and sharing information. Life and work are fun when you are paid to be who you are, a lively, outgoing extrovert.

It may take several tries before you discover the niche that is just right for you. Like Goldilocks, you have to test all the beds before you find the one that suits you. Then (surprise!) you discover that getting there was all the fun.

It's also important to recognize the five signals that let you know when you are off, way off, the passion track. As you read, make note of how many of the signals are typical of earlier stages of life. Keep in mind that it's normal to go off course. You're a human, not a saint, so don't think there is something wrong with you if these signals sound familiar. What counts is how quickly you get back on the passion path.

Off-Track Signal #1. Money Is Your Priority

The desire for money is not a sign that you are greedy. After all, you live on the earth, and you are supposed to enjoy the things that money can buy. The problem arises when money is your priority, your ultimate objective. Before you take any risk, do you want to know how much money you will make? Or is enjoying the process your goal? Remember Mike, the sales manager who kept taking high-paying jobs and then sabotaging them when he got bored? Even though he had no guarantee he would make money, Mike decided to work as a sales troubleshooter and write a book. Now he makes money, and he is rich in satisfaction.

But wait, you say, how about all those wealthy people who live in mansions? Look at the fine cars they drive, the trips and vacations, the fame and fortune. I bet they're not on the wrong track. I would sure like to trade places with them.

I don't know who you refer to, so all I can say is that you could be right, but maybe not. If wealth is the goal, you know the false self is calling the shots. You also know there is never enough money to satisfy the false self's cravings. Have you ever wondered why some people get addicted to alcohol and drugs *after* they have the villa in France, the cars, boats, trips, power, and fame? Why did material success leave them feeling so empty? Did the view from the top turn out to be a disappointment?

The top does not always give you the most accurate perspective, as was true for the fairy-tale king who had everything except food he enjoyed. When the castle cooks sent a new dish to him, the monarch took one bite and pushed the food away. Discouraged by his failure to find the dish that satisfied his picky palate, the king decided to hold a contest to find the best dish in the kingdom. The prize for the cook would be a job in the castle and a kitchen equipped with the latest medieval technology.

Heralds went out all over the kingdom with the news of the contest, and soon a long line of cooks surrounded the castle. As each cook set his dish before the king, the monarch took one bite, shoved it aside, and turned to the next cook. Cook after cook came by the throne, only to have his food rejected.

The king was so discouraged he decided to cheer himself up with a hunting expedition in the forest. While chasing a deer, the king got separated from his courtiers. He and his horse wandered through the woods all day and night. The morning of the second day, he saw smoke coming from the chimney of a woodcutter's hut. "Ah, at last," said the king as he galloped toward the hut. "Whoever lives here will know the way out of the forest."

The woodcutter was surprised to see a king at his front door, but he welcomed him into his lowly abode after giving the king's horse water and hay. "My liege, you must be starving," the woodcutter said, once he heard the king's story. He filled a platter with thick slices of freshly baked brown bread and chunks of cheese, which he put before the king.

After he had taken a few bites of the bread and cheese and washed them down with spring water, the king exclaimed, "My good man, this is the best meal I have ever eaten! You win the prize for the best dish in the kingdom."

When the woodcutter looked puzzled, the king told him about his contest to find a dish that pleased him, and that hundreds of applicants had failed to make anything he liked, until now. The woodcutter scratched his head, and then he said, "But my lord, maybe you have never been hungry before."

One can only speculate when looking from the outside at others' lavish lives. But as the woodcutter knew, you have to understand what you need before you can receive what is truly nourishing.

Off-Track Signal #2. You Worry about What Others Think

Worrying about what others think of you is a symptom of the fear of criticism. The "others" can be bosses, parents, spouses, friends, customers, or clients. When you don't get positive feedback, you assume you have done something wrong. Always assuming you have done something wrong is the result of growing up with authority figures who were perfectionists. One false move and you never heard the end of it. You were too young to know they were projecting their fear of being imperfect onto you.

Worrying about what others think can also be a holdover from adolescence, the period in life when many teenagers live and die based on what peers think, particularly popular, good-looking peers. When there is no escape from the hothouse of neurosis that constitutes middle and high school, many teenagers numb their feelings to survive the onslaught of criticism. Like Sleeping Beauty, they have to wait until the rational mind (the prince) matures to the point that it can liberate them from self-imposed slumber.

Being made fun of by the group is a fate worse than death for teens, and it is death at any age if you define public ridicule as psychological murder. Walk on any high school campus, and you'll see students dressing and talking alike so as not to stand out from the crowd. The need to belong to a peer group is a normal stage of development. Teens form bonds as a way to establish an identity apart from parents. When this stage of life is not navigated successfully, the result can be tragic. Alienated teens bring guns to school to get even with people who made fun of them, or they visit teen websites to destroy fellow teens' reputations.

If you were ever humiliated in front of a group, you know how devastating it was to your sense of worth, unless you were unusually mature. Now that you're older and wiser, you can be in a group and maintain your sense of self, unless you depend on the group to meet your emotional and security needs.

Stop and think about the groups you belonged to in the past, beginning with clubs, fraternities or sororities, companies, churches, and charitable and political organizations. Did you maintain your independence in the group, or did you give yourself up in order to be accepted?

Now think of the people whose opinions concern you. Why are they important? Can they harm you if you disagree with them? Do they worry about what others think of them? Are they quick to criticize others? Do they abandon you when others turn against you? Are they afraid to take the risks you take? If so, should these people be concerned about what you think of them?

Next, think of the people you admire and respect. Can they live without the need for agreement? Are they the same wherever they go? Are they tolerant? Do they accept mistakes as part of the creative process? Do they stand up for you when others criticize you unfairly? Is integrity the standard by which they measure behavior? Do they take the same risks you take?

You won't have to worry about people who value integrity, unless you betray your values to fit into a group. Even then, these people will forgive you, since they made the same mistake.

Off-Track Signal #3. You Focus on the End Result, Not the Process

Focusing on the end result, not where you are in the process, is another indication you have gone off the passion track. It can also mean you're in the middle stage of change, when the end is nowhere in sight and you're feeling anxious and uncertain. Getting there is all you think about, not enjoying where you are.

The need for certainty is a basic human need; an example of this need is the stock market's sensitivity to world events. The more uncertainty in the world, the more money heads for what's safe as protection from loss. The need to know what's going to happen can be so strong that you avoid risk at all costs. Better to be comfortable than sorry, you think, so you stay with what's familiar.

Risk tolerance, then, is measured by the amount of uncertainty you can handle. That's why it's important to be honest with yourself, to set small goals, and to take all the time you need to reach those goals. When you're not pushing, you don't crash when you have a setback. Moving along at a slow pace also allows you to change your mind, to alter course, to drop what you're doing for a better alternative, and to correct errors before they escalate into disasters.

Needing constant reassurance that everything will turn out well is another sign you're off the passion track. Having to be told again and again that what you're doing will succeed means you have bitten off more than you can chew. Lower your expectations until they match what you *know* you can do.

Another off-track signal is measuring success by the reward you receive when you're done, not by the change that takes place in you as you go along. You believe success comes when you finish what you're doing, not as you do the work.

Or you may have several passions, and you can't choose just one. You search websites, take classes, read books, go to seminars and retreats, follow gurus, and do what others are doing, hoping that if you throw the net wide enough you'll snag your objective. When you were younger, you needed to try everything to gain experience. You may have had mentors who guided you through the shoals of life. But now that you are older, if you're still sampling all the options and looking for guides, you're not taking advantage of what you know.

As an example of focusing on results rather than the process, imagine that one of your interests is writing. You fantasize about being a writer but you do not write. It's not the process of writing that interests you; it's the outcome. Wanting to be known as a writer is a sign that writing is not what you want to do, or that you don't know what writers do. You may think polished sentences spring from the writer's brain with no need for revision, and perfectionism stops you dead in your tracks. Or you may think you can do many other things and still write. But since passion pushes through all obstacles, including perfectionism and naïveté, another aspect of publishing may be right for you, such as sales or promoting books and authors.

My point is that no one can do many things and do them well. Even geniuses have limits. It takes ten to fifteen years to become an expert at any activity, whether you're an actor, a businessperson, an animal trainer, or an automobile mechanic. Even though life spans are longer today, there isn't enough time to master many things.

To experience what it's like to focus on one thing and do it well, look around you. Select an item to observe. Look at this object until nothing else is in your view. Don't stare at the item, just gaze. Observe the object as if you had to explain it to someone who has never seen it before. Notice the color, texture, design, and function. As you concentrate on the item, be aware of what distracts you. Do any of the six basic fears (the fear of poverty, loss of love, criticism, illness, old age, or death) clamor for your attention?

Now close your eyes, take a few deep breaths, and mentally say *relax* as you exhale. Once your mind is quiet, then think about what you want to do. Let your thoughts shift from external to internal motivation. Do this exercise every morning and night for three weeks. Minivacations from worry, such as this exercise and the focusing exercise in the previous paragraph, will train your mind to concentrate.

Many people who master their craft want to expand to new horizons. If you're an outstanding actor, for example, you may produce movies or videos. As a great cook, you may start your own television show. Or you may write bestselling cookbooks. After being a star athlete, you may become a philanthropist, funding charities that help children to build confidence. You may take one business to the top and then build another, as serial entrepreneurs do. Or you may shift into a coaching role, helping others to make their dreams come true. Life reveals opportunities when you're ready. So if you stay in tune with yourself, you'll see those doors opening, just as you'll see doors closing behind you.

Off-Track Signal #4. You Take Shortcuts to Achieve Your Objectives

Taking shortcuts is a sign that you're losing faith in the process. When a goal takes longer to reach than you expected, you look for a quicker, easier route to your objective, with a mediocre result. Taking shortcuts works in tandem with the previous off-track signal — focusing on outcomes, not where you are in the process — and (coming up next) off-track signal number 5, taking on more than you can handle. As soon as you set a goal, you can't be at peace until you cross the finish line. But as soon as you get there, you set another goal.

Is there a quick and easy way to get to any worthwhile goal? The answer is yes and no. Some shortcuts save time, like the buttons you click on your computer's editing palette, or the roads you take that bypass traffic. Another way to save time is to ask experts for advice. Those who have gone down the road you're traveling can tell you where you are, what to expect, and what to avoid. They won't tell you how long it takes, but they will say, "Be patient; don't compare yourself to others; it takes what it takes for you."

An example of a shortcut that wastes time is talking to people who aren't on the passion path. These people may make a great deal of money, be well known in their fields, and even say they're passionate about what they do. But if you listen carefully, you'll hear the false self's vanity, the craving for more and more of what the person craves, such as attention, fame, or fortune.

To know who you're really speaking to when you meet with experts, look for signs of overextension: inattentiveness, excess weight, fatigue, bad health, poor boundaries, too much traveling, an attempt to be all things to all people, concentration on money, and addictions. You'll also hear the false self's put-downs of others — and of you, if you're perceived as a threat.

Helpful experts are well aware of their limitations. They moderate their activities in order to have time to do what they love. After you talk or meet with these people, you come away feeling enlightened and encouraged. You know what you're doing wrong and how to correct the error. You also know what you're doing right.

Another shortcut to avoid is associating with people who take financial and moral shortcuts. Con artists appeal to laziness and greed, the all-too-human desire to get something without working for it. As the circus magnate P. T. Barnum once said, "There is a sucker born every minute." So beware of people who tell you there is a fast track to success.

The easy path is quick at first, and that's why it's so appealing; but then the road gets bumpier as you go along. The longer you stay on this road, the worse it gets. In some cases you wind up in jail, or dead. By contrast, the slow path is difficult at first, and that's why many people reject it. But it gets easier as you go along, because there are no gaps in your preparation.

If you stay on the hard road long enough, you sense something different going on, like during the weeks just before spring, when everything seems ready to burst into bloom. Moods of doubt and depression fade away, distractions lose their appeal, cravings subside, and hope becomes a reality not a fantasy. As you enter the third and final stage of change, you realize there are no shortcuts to excellence. Even with expert help, you have to do the work. If that were not the case, then everyone would be where you are.

You won't find as many people on the slow path to success. But those who travel that road have much in common with you. They know you do what is difficult for you and that you can't be fooled by promises that don't deliver.

Off-Track Signal #5. You Take On More Than You Can Handle

This signal is the most common cause of misery and defeat. Taking on more than you can handle causes chronic fatigue, irritability, aches and pains, and sloppy boundaries with money, work, and relationships.

Overextension is a collective as well as an individual phenomenon; witness the alarming rates of stress-related diseases, obesity, and debt. You live in a society where highly extroverted type A behavior is the norm, where the desire for more and more sensory stimulation sends countries and people over the cliff, where ruin waits at the bottom.

Spending money keeps economies humming along, but spending for what you don't need eventually destroys you and the economy. Then you work to pay debt and interest, not for pleasure. Now you have an adversarial relationship with work because you have to do it to pay your bills.

Inevitably, overextension is its own downfall, as history has proved again and again. The fall of nations and economies can be tracked back to the day leaders took on more than they could handle, promising anything to their constituents to get and stay in power or starting wars that destroyed treasuries and populations.

In every life and nation, the pendulum swings from excess to contraction, since this is how we learn. Given the condition of the world, we each need to right the imbalance in our personal lives, not add to the world's problems by doing more than we can do well. Nothing in excess, the Greek philosophers said, counsel that applies today, tomorrow, and always. Moderation is not glamorous, but it's the key to balance, collectively and individually. One person creating firm boundaries may seem like a tiny step to world peace, but a balanced life affects everyone, since we're all part of a larger whole.

Saying *no* to excess takes fortitude. Women especially are under tremendous pressure to lower their boundaries, and this pressure comes from many sources in society, such as famous role models who appear to have it all together — even if, in reality, they are exhausted and unhappy. Every Mother's Day, to give another example, women are bombarded with newspaper and magazine articles that say, "Even on Mother's Day she puts others first," as if that were the right thing to do. A more realistic and caring article would say, "Especially on Mother's Day she balances her needs with the needs of others."

If you want to succeed, double the amount of time you believe you need to reach a goal. When you catch yourself comparing yourself with others, stop. Don't worry whether they will get there before you or whether they will outdo you. They could be taking shortcuts, or someone may be making it easy for them. Or, more likely, they may be taking on more than they can handle and will soon crash and burn.

The next time someone asks you to do something, before you respond, listen to your feelings. If you override your feelings because you're afraid you're being selfish, you'll feel resentful and others will feel guilty about manipulating you (or at least they should feel guilty).

When something holds you back from reaching a goal, see frustration as a teacher that keeps you in detention until you learn your lessons. If a door closes, don't push harder against it; you'll only injure yourself. If you feel discouraged, talk about your struggle with people you trust. Contrary to what you may believe, they'll be glad to know you're human.

When all the signs say the past is over, let go. Holding on to what is dead and gone will only increase the pain. See the unknown as the friend who wants only the best for you.

Finally, when others pressure you to go too fast, too far, and too high, laugh and say that you may take longer than most people to get where you want to go, but by the time you get there, you'll really know what you're doing.

SUMMARY

1. Trust the holiness of your heart's affections.
2. Make passion, not money, your priority.
3. Focus on the process, not the outcome.
4. Be grateful for critics.
5. Work and live at your own pace.

CHAPTER 5

Create a Template for Success

Where your treasure is there your heart will be also.
— MATTHEW 6:21

Take a deep breath. You just completed an enormous task. After all, how many people do you know who have eliminated clutter and other distractions from their lives? How many have identified their life scripts, starting with a description of their grandparents' scripts about money, work, and relationships? How many are trying to change a story that always ends in failure? How many have found (or are even looking for) the authentic self, the core of the personality that sees everything just as it is? How many recognize the passion clues that indicate they're on track and the signals that indicate they are off, way off, the passion path? Now that these steps are behind *you*, the next step is to create a template for success.

A template is a form that ensures the same outcome every time you use it. Similarly, a template for success helps you to make choices that work for you and to avoid the choices that will never work. As a group, your strengths, values, needs, and temperament are your template for success. Referring to this template when you have to make an important decision increases your chances for success. For example, when you know your temperament, you know what energizes you. If you're an introvert, you turn down invitations to large gatherings because they sap your energy. But you accept invitations from one person or to join a small group, because intimacy recharges your batteries. If you know you're an extrovert, you join networking groups and clubs, and you go to conferences, large gatherings, and parties, because you get charged up around people.

Temperament remains the same throughout your life, but your strengths, values, and needs change over time, so you need to know what's true for you at this stage of life. As an example, you once thought you were strong when you saved people from the consequences of their poor choices. Now you know that being strong means letting people experience consequences. You used to value status, how you looked in the eyes of people you thought were important. You wanted to be out and about so you wouldn't miss opportunities to be seen and known by these people. Now creativity is your top value, so you limit exposure in order to concentrate on the project at hand. In the past you needed others to validate your perceptions. Now that you're confident, all you need is to trust the process.

Your awareness of who you are and what you value and need increases over time and with experience. But developmentally speaking, midlife is when you become more of who you were designed to be.

Awareness

By definition, awareness means that you're sensitive to what's going on inside you and in your environment. Unless you numb yourself with addictions or excessive activity, your sensitivity heightens as you age, which is why you make wiser choices.

In their classic textbook, *Theories of Personality*, psychologists Calvin Hall and Gardner Lindzey discuss Jung's comments about the unfolding of awareness, a process that accelerates during midlife, Jung says, if earlier stages have been navigated successfully. According to Hall and Lindzey:

Before a self can emerge it is necessary for the various compo-
nents of the personality to become fully developed and individu-
ated. For this reason, the archetype of the self does not become
evident until the person has reached middle age. At this time, he [or
she] begins to make a serious effort to change the center of the
personality from the conscious ego to one that is midway between
consciousness and subconsciousness. This midway region is the
province of the self.[1]

Hall and Lindzey summarize Jung's analysis of what happens to an
individual when the normal shift of life energy in midlife is blocked because of unresolved trauma or any of the six basic fears: the fear of
poverty, criticism, loss of love, illness, old age, or death. This is when
an unfolding story gets interrupted:

When an individual reaches the late thirties or early forties a rad-
ical [change in values] occurs. Youthful interests and pursuits lose
their value and are replaced by new interests which are more cultural and less biological.... This transition is the most decisive
event in a person's life. It is also one of the most hazardous because if anything goes amiss during the transference of energy the
personality may become permanently crippled. This happens, for
example, when the cultural and spiritual values of middle age do
not utilize all of the energy formerly invested in instinctual aims.
In that case the excess energy is free to upset the equilibrium of the
psyche. Jung had a great deal of success treating middle-age people whose energies have failed to find satisfying outlets [passion in
midlife and beyond!].[2]

By transference of energy from instinctual to spiritual aims, Jung
means that sexual energy formerly used to conquer the outside world
or to attract partners is channeled into creative outlets in midlife, since
we are past the stage of procreation. These outlets give the second half
of life meaning and purpose. Continuing to use libidinal energy to
achieve sexual and material goals causes the psychic disturbance that
Jung describes: the midlife crisis mentioned in the introduction to this
book, with its accompanying feelings of alienation and depression.

To restore balance to the personality, individuals need to redirect libidinal energy to goals that bring emotional and spiritual fulfillment. In midlife the mind naturally turns inward to find meaning and purpose, the "serious effort" Jung describes. Becoming more introverted, then, indicates that you're in sync with the rhythms of life.

You began the inner journey to find your authentic self when you eliminated the distractions from your life. Then you wrote your life story, a heroic effort that, as Jung says, shifted the center of your personality from the conscious ego to the province of the self.

Think of the self as the chairperson of a board of directors. Each director (aspect of the personality) is welcome, no matter how bleak or pie-in-the-sky its viewpoint. But no director is allowed to dominate and control, since balance is the self's objective, meaning the separate parts of you fit together to form a harmonious or credible whole.

Ah, but just when you think you have it all together, something happens that causes you to lose your balance. Perhaps you accept an invitation to a large, noisy group, or you take on projects that you don't have the energy to do well. Oh no, you say to yourself, I thought I was done with that. But by now you know to accept relapse as normal, since the script's roots reach deep into your subconscious and into the collective mind you share. It is only logical that sometimes you'll have to go deeper before you can continue forward.

The Collective Mind

The collective mind was portrayed brilliantly as the Borg on the television series *Star Trek: The Next Generation*. Huge blocky spaceships filled with robotlike beings roamed the universe to absorb individuals into the collective. "Resistance is futile; you will be assimilated," members of the Borg chanted in unison as they descended on other planets or spaceships. Those who valued the right to make choices fought against being turned into machines linked to a master brain, the scriptwriter's analogy for the individual who resists "group think."

Captain Jean-Luc Picard and the crew of the *Enterprise* undertook many life-and-death battles before they put the Borg out of the assimilation business, at least for the duration of the television series. Similarly, you go through a life-and-death struggle when you challenge collective scripts about money, work, and relationships. Optimism, then, can trigger profound pessimism.

For example, the poet Yeats said the Irish have an abiding sense of tragedy that sustains them through temporary periods of joy. His wry description of the Victim mentality was also a theme in the works of the Irish writer James Joyce. Joyce's stories are populated with people whose stories always end in failure, his way of expressing his exasperation with the Irish tendency to give power to a higher authority (the church, England, alcohol) rather than exercise their own power.

Like artists and all others who see deeply, Joyce broke through the denial in his culture with an honest appraisal of personal and collective motives. Joyce had his own addictions to alcohol and despair. But the difference between the ordinary person and the genius is that the latter transforms personal experience into work that rings true for everyone.[3] Although alcohol consumption remains high in Ireland, today it's a better place than it was during the time of Joyce and Yeats, thanks to educational opportunities and religious and political freedom. Nowhere are people perfect, but Ireland's citizens who learn from poor judgment can now hope for a better future.

Like the Irish, your collective forebearers may have been wary of apparent happy endings if they lived in countries influenced by the Puritans or other extreme religions. The literal interpretation of religious texts made perfection, not happiness, the goal, and if you were enjoying life and succeeding, you were no doubt in league with the devil. If you were striving to be perfect and failing, then you were on the path to salvation.

You won't find much happiness in Russian or European novels or plays, either, although you will find brutal honesty about what it's like to suffer under religious, royal, and state tyranny. Asian, Arab, and

African cultures have their own brand of collective pessimism: rigid family and political structures, religious fanaticism, tribal warfare, hordes of vandals terrorizing the countryside, and cruel despots destroying everything in sight. It's a miracle anything works at all, given the irrational side of human nature.

Human history appears to be an ongoing struggle between the proponents of freedom and the proponents of totalitarian systems, individually and collectively. Freedom is always the harder choice because it places responsibility on the individual. Centralized power is seductive because people can blame those in charge when things go wrong ("If it weren't for you . . .").

Tyrants from ancient times to the present have come to power by promising utopian outcomes. Just give us control, they say, and we will solve your problems (the assumption is that citizens can't do it themselves). By contrast, those who offer freedom don't promise anything except the right to make choices and learn from them (the assumption is the citizens will).

Those who have learned from history know that inner transformation precedes outer change, not the other way around. This is why top-down attempts to improve human nature are doomed to fail, no matter how well intended.

Self-transformation is a hard row to hoe if you're the only member of your family who is interested in changing and growing, as was true for Ann (described in the first chapter). She thought if she let go and stopped trying to control everyone, everything would fall apart. The truth was just the opposite: good boundaries saved her marriage and her sanity. Of course, some relationships will end when you change, but healthier relationships will take their place.

Personal growth feels similar to the way you feel when you survive a tragedy that kills others, or when others suffer losses and you don't — or, on a less cosmic note, when your life works and others' lives are an ongoing soap opera. Do these people ask how you got where you are? Probably not, if they assume that growth comes without effort. According to some, failure, whether collective or individual, is never the Victim's fault, whether the Victim is a person or a country. There's a demon out there making life harder for them than it is for you. If it were not for . . . (fill in the blank), they would be as happy and successful as you.

Change really annoys some people. They would rather stick with what they know, even if it kills them in the process. No doubt you encountered resistance when you stopped "helping" people who kept making bad choices. Some of them got angry with you when you gave up the Rescuer role; others accused you of not caring about them. If you fell for this ploy, you went back to rescuing them, and then you felt angry and resentful (ah, now you're back home again).

After enough defeats you admitted that you had a problem, and you asked for help if you needed it. Then you moved into the second stage of change, being patient while you practiced making healthy choices. Most likely, when change took longer than you expected, you gave up — and then you fell into a depression. "What's the use," you thought. "I've done it again; I might as well quit." Then you pulled yourself out of the pit of despair and tried again, and again, until you reached the third and final stage of change, when choices that work became the path of least resistance. You still keep an eye on your flaws, however, since you know complacency is your worst enemy.

Now that I have recapped the three stages of change, let's create your template for success, beginning with what you do easily and well.

Strengths

Your strengths are what you do naturally, seemingly without effort. By *natural* I don't mean what's easy. Giving birth to a creative project is natural when you're creative, but it's not easy. You have to struggle to bring forth anything new and original. Just ask any mother.

What is natural is a talent you have worked on until it *looks* easy, like a champion tennis player's backhand, an Olympic ice skater's triple jump, an actor's flawless interpretation, an editor's eagle eye, a masseur's healing touch, or the ease with which you relate to children and other people or complicated systems. After a great deal of time and effort, you don't even think about what you're doing; you just do it, like brushing your teeth every morning. Because your strengths are so natural, however, you may assume that everyone can do what you do and that these strengths have no special value.

Taking strengths for granted makes it hard for you to identify what comes naturally to you. Like muscles in a well-trained body, your strengths respond with ease to challenge, so easily you may even feel guilty about getting paid for these strengths (this is the Puritan legacy again). For example, are you intuitive? Do you grasp the meaning of a situation without using deductive logic? Do you have flashes of insight that later turn out to be uncannily accurate? Are people startled by the information that comes to you seemingly from out of nowhere? Are you always ahead of your time? If so, intuition is one of your strengths, what you do naturally and well.

Earlier in life you probably doubted your intuition. When people asked how you knew what you knew, it was hard to come up with an answer. Some thought you were crazy, out of touch with the world of facts and figures. Because you believed they knew more than you, you doubted intuition's revelations. Then you did go crazy, since denied intuition erupts as mood swings, anxiety attacks, and bouts of depression. If you visit an insane asylum, a totalitarian state, or a religious fanatic, you will see the havoc wreaked by repressed intuition.

Later (sometimes *much* later), when time proved you intuited the right answer, you felt amazed and relieved. I guess I'm not crazy after all, you said to yourself. You promised yourself that next time you wouldn't doubt yourself. However, it was years before you were comfortable with intuition's power. This is an example of how strengths develop over time and with use.

To feel free, useful, and creative, you need to get paid for using your intuition. You make your greatest contribution when you reveal to others what is obvious to you, such as a new way to use their resources or a way they can improve what they're doing. The ability to tune into intuition's otherworldly signals helps employers, clients, and customers to connect the dots between the past, today, and what's coming in the future. Can you see how marketable intuition is a problem-solving skill? Who would pay for intuition's remarkable foresight? Would you?

Honesty is another strength that grows over time and with experience. Because of a fear of authority, you may have held back what you thought and felt when you were younger. But after you graduated from the school of hard knocks, you were not afraid to tell it like it is. Who would benefit from honesty's humor and X-ray vision? Would you?

Like all strengths, patience develops the more you use it. You're tested throughout life to see if impatience will get the best of you; and it does, until you interpret setbacks and delays as opportunities to reflect, review, and revise. Patience prefers slow, steady progress since that's the path to excellence. How important is the ability to be patient with the process, any process, to know that your best effort is worth the wait? Who wants to buy the crafted, as opposed to the rushed, result? Do you?

Intuition, honesty, and patience often accompany courage, since this strength is based on a sense of timing. Courage is not the absence of fear, nor is it foolhardiness. Boldness acts in the face of fear, but not without sizing up the consequences. Who would pay someone who is courageous enough to tell the truth in spite of the risks? Would you?

It has been said that we stay poor because we buy cheap things and buy too many of them, rather than wait until we can purchase items that last. Immediate gratification feels good at first, but soon what we bought on impulse wears out, or it's not what we need. Thus, judgment is another strength that increases with time. Who will gladly pay for good judgment? Will you?

If you prefer quality, not quantity, in your work, relationships, and belongings; character more than wealth or fame; the simple as opposed to the complicated; caution rather than haste; and your own approval over the approval of others, then judgment is one of your strengths. Now let's determine what you think is important at this stage of life.

Values

Your values are where your treasure is, meaning your heart's desire. Advertising, media, and popular icons can influence values, but in the end only you know what will make you happy. Your values change as you age, although some values may remain constant all through your life. For example, once you thought it was cool to keep up with the latest fashion trends. Now you value comfort and styles that don't go out of style. If you still value variety, however, you continue to enjoy a wide spectrum of people and experiences.

When your values, or those of others, change, people enter or leave your life either gradually or abruptly. Or you may be the one who does the entering and leaving. You may not know that separation is the result of changing values; perhaps all you know is that you're intrigued with someone new or are no longer intrigued with someone else. Values attract people and circumstances, and they send them away.

Sometimes a person's values are in transition, as was the case for Julie (discussed in chapters 2 and 3). She was torn between starting her own business and staying with her job because of security needs, even though conflicts with her boss kept her awake at night. Conflicts that keep you awake at night indicate the subconscious is getting restless. You had better take action, or the creative self will arrange it so that you leave with fireworks, or you may set things up so that others force you to end what you've outgrown.

Sometimes leaving is not the solution. For example, perhaps you need to be more assertive. If assertiveness solves the problem, the subconscious calms down and you sleep well at night. In Julie's case, she needed to get her emotions under control and to stop doing more than was comfortable for her quiet temperament. In the meantime, she went through the remaining steps in this book.

Mike (introduced in chapter 3) needed to resolve his conflict between creativity and money. As he wrote his story, Mike realized that frequent family moves had conditioned him to like change and flexibility, which was one of his top strengths. (This is an example of the insight you gain as you write your story: you see what you could not see before.) Mike used to think he was flaky and unreliable because he liked change, but in truth he was bored after he figured out the solution to a problem. Yet he interpreted boredom as a lack of commitment, and so did his bosses.

Mike was a project type, not a maintainer, the type of worker companies need in order to keep their operations running smoothly. You can see why corporations have a hard time keeping people like Mike happy: they must keep putting them at the bottom of learning curves. But few companies can keep funding internal start-ups — the development stage of products and services cuts into profits, which makes the stockholders unhappy. In the end, awareness solved Mike's career problem. "I was making this too complicated," he said. "I have to be in a start-up."

This is another example of how you can know something intellectually, but until you know it emotionally you remain stuck in the past. Once Mike's subconscious accepted that being a project person was the best use of his strengths, he found the right niche.

Well, that's fine for Julie and Mike, you say, but how do I know what comes naturally to me? And who's going to pay me for those strengths, especially when the economy falters? And by the way, how long will it take to find my niche — I'm not getting any younger, you know — and once I get there, will I keep succeeding? Good questions, and they all indicate the need for certainty.

Of necessity, the stories I tell in this book compress a long process into a few pages, so don't think Mike and Julie found perfect niches in a few months. It took time for them to let go of the fear and self-doubt that held them back from success. For example, Julie had to stop feeling guilty when she said no to what was not right for her. Mike had to root out the belief that he was not good enough. A recurring dream revealed that a lack of confidence was his problem. In his dream Mike kept going back to graduate school to finish one last class. In reality, he already had a graduate degree in business, but subconsciously he thought of himself as a student, which attracted bosses who agreed with his low opinion of himself.

As with Mike and Julie, once you trust the process — and you must tolerate the slowness with which the subconscious accepts the new as true — you have already found the goose that lays the golden eggs. It's just a matter of time before they hatch. Your next question should be: "What do I need in order to reach my full potential?"

Needs

You may not know what you need, but you probably know what you want. The difference between a want and a need is that you can get along without a want, but a need is what you must have to feel fulfilled, as you are when you eat a balanced, nutritious diet as opposed to eating junk food. No doubt there were times when you were glad you did not get what you wanted in the past, since that was not what you needed. For example, you thought you were madly in love with someone, and when that didn't work out you were crushed. A few years later you realized you didn't even like that person. Or you thought you had to have the latest style of clothing, and then those clothes went out of fashion the following year.

When genuine needs are met, you feel good about yourself and life in general. Daily life is rich with meaning then, as opposed to the frustration you feel when you don't get what you need. Think of a need as nourishment for a plant. Wouldn't life be simple if you had been born with a list of your needs attached, like the care tag on a plant in a nursery? Give the child this at this age and that at that age, and it will bloom; and don't give the child this at all, or it will wither away. Of course this presumes you would have had parents or caretakers who followed wise advice.

Fortunately, you are like both the plant and the gardener who can help you grow to your full potential. But embarrassment about doing what you love may be an obstacle. For example, when I asked Mike to put the word *creativity* on his list of needs, he looked embarrassed. "Aha, I think we just discovered a need," I said to Mike when I saw this, and we laughed. He felt uncomfortable with the word *creativity* because expressing emotion in work was okay for artists, but not for a hard-nosed sales executive. This is an example of negative beliefs about work that have been passed down through the generations.

After a few weeks, Mike said he was becoming more comfortable seeing himself as creative. "I've always liked to improve things, like starting new sales territories," he said. "And I have my own style of communicating to my customers. I don't know why I couldn't see that as being creative."

What need do you have that you feel embarrassed about admitting? Are you embarrassed about needing a quiet place where you can work without interruption? Or are you embarrassed about needing to work with a partner or teammates? To get over feelings of embarrassment, ask yourself who besides you benefits when your needs are met. How would fulfillment of your needs help the world to be a better place?

Your needs may not have been met when you were young, or even in more recent times. In fact, others may have made fun of you for having needs, especially emotional needs, so you pretended you didn't have needs. Ridicule is the chief enemy of passion, because it destroys self-confidence, the ability to ask for what you need without shame or embarrassment. So be selective when and with whom you share your heart's desire. Many a wonderful idea has died at birth because of critics who ridiculed what they didn't understand.

Now, before you can make a list of your needs, you must distinguish between needs and craving, the constant longing for what never satisfies.

Craving

Remember the story about the king whose appetite was never satisfied? That was a case of craving versus needs. The king craved an exquisitely tasty dish, when what he needed was an empty stomach. Have you ever craved something or someone? Did you believe that until you got what you craved, you could not be satisfied? Did you want what you craved so badly that it was all you could think about? When you got what you craved — a relationship, a possession, or someone's approval — did you feel satisfied? Or did you crave more and more and more?

Painful craving, or *tanha*, to use the Buddhist term, is based on human vanity, whereas true needs come from the authentic self. Craving is a cruel hoax, according to Vernon Howard, the author of *The Power of Your Supermind*.[4] His thesis is that the problem of craving can be resolved only by clear thinking (the prince!). Howard's term *supermind* refers to a state of mind that is free from attachment. From that lofty point of view, your goals are more practical than a chair, your vision that of an eagle perching in peaceful contentment on a mountaintop.

By contrast, Howard says, craving "is a cunning thief of life force [chi] that fools you into thinking itself necessary for your existence, while all the time it steals genuine existence."[5] Fictitious appetites can be recognized and ignored, Howard points out. The next time your mind is obsessing about something you crave, stand aside and observe what's going on, as though you're watching a movie that interests you. If you can separate yourself from the mental anguish for even a moment, you'll have experienced the power of the supermind.

Howard says that when we hear the truth, either the false or the true self hears it. The false self rejects, distorts, or ignores what does not agree with its limited viewpoint, like a person whose mind is closed. The authentic self, on the other hand, is eager for the truth because it provides understanding and relief (as when it says to itself, "Oh, *that's* why I am not succeeding").[6]

Maddeningly, what the false self craves is the opposite of what the authentic self needs, as when you crave invitations to travel to faraway places when what you really need is to go to a retreat. Howard cites examples of mystics throughout the ages who experienced the bliss that follows release from the torment of craving. Strangely enough, he says, the problem is that we fear the very quietness we seek. "Desire only what is truly necessary," he writes. "But *there* is where we must throw every ounce of insight into the battle. We must distinguish between true and false needs. Otherwise we condemn ourselves to the butterfly life, forever flittering and never resting. Rather than trying to escape a dilemma," he advises, "have a passion for understanding it."[7]

Understanding is not just knowledge, as when you know where a place is on the globe and its history. Understanding is knowledge plus the ability to empathize with any situation. Shakespeare had knowledge, but it was his empathy for the human condition that allowed him to create the characters who became archetypes. The personalities in Shakespeare's plays are so authentic that it's hard to imagine Iago, Hamlet, Juliet, or Falstaff as the products of an author's imagination. Throughout the world, they are embedded in the collective subconscious for now and always, separate from the modest man called William Shakespeare.

As an experiment, pretend you're an actor auditioning for the role of your false self. To get the job, you have to become the part of you that is motivated by vanity (the part who says things like, "If I had this, then I would feel important"). How do you convince the audience that this is who you are? What will you do and say? What will you never do or say? Who are the supporting actors surrounding the false self?

Now set aside the false self's vanity for the moment. Imagine you're an actor auditioning for the role of your authentic self. How do you convince the audience that you are the authentic you? What will you do and say? What will you never do or say? Who are the supporting actors surrounding your authentic self? Maslow's hierarchy of needs will help you see where you are on the path to self-actualization.

Maslow's Hierarchy of Needs

Abraham Maslow was a psychologist who studied healthy people, as opposed to those who were mentally ill or neurotic. Some of the people he observed were famous, such as Albert Einstein and Eleanor Roosevelt. He also studied individuals from the healthiest 1 percent of the college student population. Based on his sample of healthy people, Maslow devised a hierarchy of needs that he portrayed as a pyramid, with survival needs at the bottom. Above those are safety needs. Next are social needs: love and friendship. As you go up the pyramid, you reach ego needs: self-respect, personal worth, and autonomy. At the peak of Maslow's pyramid is the need for self-actualization, the desire to become the best one can be.[8]

Survival needs are physiological: we need shelter, food, air, and warmth. Obviously these are "must haves," not cravings. However, it's possible to meet survival needs and still crave more food or shelter than you need. What you *need* in this case is further up the pyramid: higher self-esteem.

The next higher stage in Maslow's hierarchy is *security* needs: safety and protection from danger. Children need parents to protect them from harm, just as you need police and locks on your door to protect you from criminals. But you can be safe and still feel a sense of impending doom. In this case, you need to distinguish fact from irrational fear, today from yesterday. If you make carelessness your enemy, then you feel secure.

After survival and security needs come *social* needs: friendship, love, romantic as well as familial and committed love, and a sense of belonging. You can have your social needs met and still be in need of a true friend, someone who loves you enough to tell you what you don't want to hear. You will recognize this person after you finish the work in this chapter. You will also know whom *not* to call friend.

As the pyramid narrows to the top, you come to what Maslow calls ego needs. He means the healthy ego's needs, not the false self's cravings. The ego's needs are self-respect, personal worth, and autonomy.

You feel secure when you can provide yourself with shelter, food, and warmth. You feel safe when you know that you'll make wise choices. If your social needs are met, you have self-respect, a sense of worth, and autonomy. Now you come to the tip of Maslow's pyramid, the need for self-actualization. Maslow defines this as the successful use of talent and skills (the theme of this book). Here are traits of self-actualized people:

- They embrace the facts and realities of the world instead of denying or avoiding them.
- They are spontaneous in their ideas and actions.
- They are creative.
- They are interested in solving problems; this often includes the problems of others. Solving these problems is often a key focus in their lives.
- They feel a connection to other people and generally appreciate life.
- They have a system of morality that is fully internalized and independent of external authority.
- They have discernment and are able to view all things objectively.

Fully functioning individuals are rare, according to Maslow, since they act purely on their own volition (remember Holt's discussion of internal motivation in chapter 3?). As the list implies, such individuals see themselves as distinct and whole, yet not separate from their fellow humans.[9]

I see spiritual needs as belonging to Maslow's hierarchy of needs, since the need for faith, tranquility of spirit, and a connection with the Divine make life worth living no matter where you are on Maslow's pyramid of needs. The apostle Paul is an example of what it's like to be content at all times and in all places. "I know both how to be abased and to abound," he said while in prison (Philippians 4:11–12). Lao-tzu, the founder of Taoism, is another model of happiness in the midst of upheaval. The Taoist's philosophy is to flow with events, working in harmony with what happens in daily life, not resisting, defending, or trying to change the inevitable.

Flowing with daily events does not mean that you allow others to infringe on your rights, or that you're out of touch with what's going on in the world. On the contrary, the difference between denial and living "the Way" is a happy serenity and a subtle sense of humor.[10]

Now let's examine some examples of strengths, values, and needs.

Examples of Strengths, Values, and Needs

If I were to drop you off in a strange town, you would immediately start using your strengths. Let's say organization is one of your strengths, something that comes naturally to you after years of practice. How will this strength reveal itself after I leave you in the new town?

Do you stop and think before you take action? Do you research the town, businesses, or whatever else you're interested in before you jump into anything? What else is true about you as an organized person? If you're organized, you're likely to be focused. When you're focused, you're efficient, and when you're efficient you're reliable. When you're reliable, people trust you.

For other clues, ask yourself what you do when you're internally motivated. What gives you the most personal satisfaction? What do people always say about you in an admiring way? Just as important, how does using these strengths help others? What circumstances call forth your strengths like well-trained soldiers? Given the following strengths, what could a person do for others, both in a crisis and in ordinary times?

- Intuition
- Honesty
- Patience
- Courage
- Judgment

Now imagine you're an employer, a client, or a customer. Even though you have no résumé for this individual and know nothing else about her, what can you imagine someone with this combination of strengths doing for you? What difficulties could she overcome, seemingly without effort?

Next, imagine that these strengths belong to you (you can identify your strengths later). Where would you be productive? Where would you be unproductive? Can you see that knowing your strengths eliminates choices that don't use your strengths?

Your Five Strengths and Values

Make a list of your top five strengths, what you do easily and well after a lifetime of experience. If you'd like help assembling this list, you can send an email to people who know you well: friends, bosses, clients, customers, family members, friends, and coworkers, along with a note letting them know what you're doing and why you value their view of you. Most people like to get involved in the journey to passion. And who knows, you may inspire them to figure out what they do naturally and well too. Following is a sample of what you might say in your email.

STRENGTHS-YOU-SEE EMAIL

Hello _____,

I'm in the process of identifying my strengths, what I do naturally and well. Because I may take these strengths for granted, I'd like to know what you think comes naturally to me — what you believe I don't even have to think about when I'm doing something but instead just do it.

Thanks for your help, and if you'd like me to email a list of the things I think you do easily and well, let me know.

Your Name

To gain more insight into strengths you may take for granted, study the following list. Do any of these strengths describe you?

- Is a quick thinker
- Has a sense of humor
- Is a leader
- Gets to the point
- Learns quickly
- Is good with her (or his) hands
- Is inspired when working alone
- Is inspired when working with one other person
- Is inspired when working with or in front of a group

Now you're ready to select your top five values. Some values may be new to you; others will be what you've always valued. Don't pick a value simply because you think you should have that value or because someone you admire has it.

- Security: the need to know, certainty, predictability
- Status: how you appear in the eyes of others
- Compensation: money and/or benefits for services rendered
- Achievement: mastery of a task, the ability to do a project well
- Advancement: improving and progressing
- Affiliation: the need to associate with like-minded people
- Recognition: special notice or attention for individual or team effort
- Authority: the power or right to command, direct, and manage
- Independence: freedom from the control of others
- Altruism: concern for the welfare of others
- Creativity: finding new, improved ways of doing anything
- Ethical harmony: your moral values are reinforced in the work setting
- Intellectual stimulation: the need for people and work that encourage thinking
- Variety: diversity of activities, people, and tasks
- Aesthetics: love of the beautiful and the sublime[11]

After you select your values, you may realize another value is a better fit. Good. Keep in mind that what you do consistently is what you value. Keep working with the list until the values feel authentic. Let's say you chose the following five values:

1. Independence
2. Creativity
3. Intellectual stimulation
4. Variety
5. Aesthetics

Do these values represent what you do now, or are they what you want to do? As an example, do you work well now without supervision, or do you need structures and guidelines to follow? If so, then you need predictability (security), at least for now. Needing structures and guidelines also indicates that you would reach your full potential when working for someone else rather than when working by yourself. As I said, be honest; don't try to be what you're not.

But suppose you notice that the more control you have over your time, the more productive you are. If so, then independence is a value. If you chafe at rules and regulations, find them restrictive, and are more productive when you set your own rules, then you value creativity. Again, the values you choose are what you need in order to become the best you can be; no particular value is better or worse than the others. And, as you grow in confidence, your values will change. Psychologist Carl Rogers says there is a correlation between growth and flexibility: "For healthy, integrated adjustment one must constantly be evaluating his experiences to see whether they require a change in the value structure. Any fixed set of values will tend to prevent the person from reacting effectively to new experiences. One must be flexible in order to adjust appropriately to the changing conditions of life."[12] When your values change, you adjust accordingly rather than wait for the outside world to jolt you into awareness. For a greater understanding of strengths and values, define what they mean to you, as in the following example.

My five strengths:

1. Intuition lets me grasp the big picture.
2. Honesty keeps me grounded in reality.
3. Patience builds faith in the process.
4. Courage forces me to take risks.
5. Judgment gives me discernment.

My five values:

1. Independence lets me control my destiny.
2. Creativity is the outlet for my emotions.
3. Intellectual stimulation exercises my mental muscles.
4. Variety broadens my point of view.
5. Aesthetics nourishes my soul.

Your lists are probably different from the above examples, or maybe they are similar. Note how changing even one value changes what you need. After Julie chose independence, she knew she would never be happy until she worked on her own. Once Mike replaced security with creativity, he realized he would do his best in a start-up situation.

Your Top Five Needs

Sometimes strengths, values, and needs are the same: you are creative, you value creativity, and you need to be creative. The way to express creativity as a need is to describe what you need in order to be creative. For example, unstructured time, solitude, and self-discipline are pre-requisites for creativity. If you have aesthetics on your list of values, as in the earlier example, you need a beautiful, orderly environment. When aesthetics is not one of your values, then being surrounded by beauty and order is not a priority.

Now let's discover your temperament needs. First, rank your introversion or extroversion on a scale of one to ten, with one being the most introverted and ten the most extroverted. The number you select indicates the amount of time you need to be alone and with others. For example, if you choose five, then you need to be alone half the time. Remember that introversion is not a matter of being withdrawn or antisocial, nor is extroversion the state of being "on" to the point of being manic. Your authentic temperament is determined at the moment of conception. Trouble starts when you try to be somebody you were not designed to be.

For example, most people thought Julie was an extrovert because she got along well with people. But chronic fatigue indicated that she was spending far too much time with people. To reach her full potential, Julie needed to work alone on design projects for clients and on the house she was remodeling. Her interaction would be with her clients and the building contractor. Here are Julie's strengths, values, and needs.

STRENGTHS

Creativity/design
Business skill
Resourcefulness
Problem solving
Complex project management

NEEDS OR VALUES

Autonomy: independence, freedom of expression
Aesthetic and emotional connection with my art
Intellectual and creative challenges
Connection with my customers
Project diversity
Feeling of completion
Integrity in my work: quality over quantity

You can see why being a manager in a large corporation was the wrong niche for Julie. Now that she's in her perfect niche, she's the secure, balanced individual that Maslow places at the top of his pyramid.

Your Template for Success

Your template for success describes the niche where you will exceed your own and others' expectations. There, you will make the money you need, and you will reach your full potential.

Begin by making a list of your top five strengths. Next to this list write, "These are the strengths others need from me to achieve their objectives." Alongside your list of five values write, "My ideal customer (or client or employer) has most or all of these values." Next to the list of your five needs write, "I am happy when these needs are met."

Julie is happy when she serves customers who value what she has to offer. They're happy because Julie meets their design needs. Do you see the concept of mutual benefit here, that Julie's template for success is also a template for her customers' success?

To remind yourself of your template for success, write your strengths, values, needs, and temperament on a three-by-five card. On the opposite side of the card, list the five passion clues (which you determined in chapter 4) on the left side of the card and the five off-track signals on the right side. The next time you have to make an important decision, such as signing a business agreement or choosing a friend or an investment advisor, refer to this list.

When choices consistently match your template for success, you reach the top of Maslow's pyramid: self-actualization. As a self-directed, fully functioning individual, you transform your world into a better place.

SUMMARY

1. What are your strengths?
2. What are your values?
3. What do you need?
4. What is your temperament?
5. Who benefits from your template for success?

CHAPTER 6

Take Small Steps

Patience, money and time bring all things to pass.
— GEORGE HERBERT

You remember how you felt before you took your first step into the unknown. It was hard to admit that what you were doing was not working and to ask for help if you needed it. But you did it because the alternative, doing nothing, was worse. At that point you may have hired a coach or counselor to help you stay on the passion path, or you may have joined forces with a passion buddy to keep you accountable.

The next step was to identify and face the fears that kept you up at night: the fear of poverty, criticism, loss of love, illness, old age, or death. Now that these ghosts are out of your subconscious, they are not the frightening ogres they used to be.

The next step into the unknown was to eliminate everything from your surroundings except what you love and use. With clutter and out-dated possessions out of the way, you could concentrate on writing your life story, paying attention to choices that turned out well and choices that did not. As you wrote, you became aware of your script, the story that always ended in failure, as in the movie *Groundhog Day*. Now you find that, more and more, healthy choices are becoming the path of least resistance for you. When you find yourself playing roles in the Drama

Triangle, whether Victim, Rescuer, or Persecutor, you say to yourself, "This is a game that goes nowhere, and I choose not to play."

The next steps into the unknown introduced you to five passion clues and five off-track signals. Next you discovered your strengths, values, needs, and temperament. Now that you have a template for success, you are ready to set realistic goals. What do I mean by *realistic*? For some people that word implies "no fun." Okay, I'm grown up now, so I have to give up my dreams and settle for what I can get. Is that true? Or is reality something that will make you feel happy and content?

Think of the opposite of reality: illusion. How fun is this charlatan? Do you remember when you were caught up in fantasies and how disappointed you felt when what you thought was real turned out to be an illusion? Was crashing down to earth fun? You were not aware that the reason you failed in the past was because your goals were unrealistic. Had you known how hard you would have to work to change these choices, you might not have started this journey.

Change that lasts is, of necessity, a slow, gradual process. The subconscious needs time to consolidate gains. The human mind is designed to incorporate learning in small doses. Over time, learning becomes cumulative, as every good teacher knows. For example, say your goal is economic independence. This goal is too vague and too big, so you are bound to fail. However, if you specify what you *mean* by economic independence, you can design the first and remaining steps that will get you to your goal. First, ask why you want to reach this goal — what will you do when you get there?

If your answer is that you want financial freedom so that you can do what you want to do, you are breaking the first "law" of money, which is to do what you love and *then* the money will come. How the money comes can't be predicted. But come it does, in ways that will surprise you. Obviously, if you're deep in debt and out of money, you need to get out of debt and make money. While you're climbing out of the hole, set small goals you can reach each day, since this will build confidence.

Bill Parcells, a former coach in the National Football League, used the small-step approach to turn around terrible teams in surprisingly short order. Two of his teams went on to win Super Bowls; several others got to the playoffs. Before Parcells came on the scene, players on the teams he was to coach focused on getting to the Super Bowl, which is why they never got there, just as people who focus on getting rich, and not on what they want to do, fail to reach their goals. Parcells taught the players to concentrate on making the *down* they were in, not the quarter, the half, the game, or the next game. His experience with players taught him three basic rules of leadership:

First, he says, you must be brutally honest with people. The only way to change people, he discovered, was to tell them what they were doing wrong. If they didn't want to listen, they didn't belong on the team.

Parcells's second rule of leadership is to confront others with their mistakes. Confrontation is necessary and healthy, he says, a critical function of turning around any organization or person. This does not mean you humiliate people — that will put you in the role of the Persecutor. Instead, you must be respectful and firm, letting others know that you want them to succeed. If you want to get the most out of people, he says, you have to be truthful, since people respond to the direct approach. As proof, his players say that what they remember most about Parcells is his statement "I think you are better than you think you are."[1]

Parcells's third rule of leadership is to set and reach small goals. When people set small, visible goals, he says, and they achieve them, they get it into their heads (their subconscious) that they can succeed. They break the mental habit that causes them to lose, and this gets them into the habit of winning.

Note that Parcells's process is similar to the one you use when you change a self-destructive life script. First be brutally honest with yourself: admit that what you're doing is not working, and ask for help if you need it. Then persevere through the middle stage of change until you reach the third and final stage: when the subconscious accepts the new as logical.

Here's how you can use Parcells's three rules for self-change:

1. Be brutally honest with yourself.
2. Don't be afraid of self-confrontation; it's necessary and healthy.
3. Take small steps that get you in the habit of succeeding.

Joanna's Story

Joanna is a client who learned the importance of taking small steps. This was difficult for her because she had a habit of taking on more than she could handle and then getting angry when she failed. By now you know this is a script, a story that always ends in failure. You also know Joanna was playing the role of the Victim in the Drama Triangle.

By all external standards, Joanna was successful. She had two advanced degrees in health administration. Her father, a physician, and her mother, a nurse, both encouraged Joanna to pursue a career in health, and they paid for her education. She held a series of senior positions in public health, yet she was frustrated by the slowness of decision making and by the political infighting. By the time her ideas were implemented, they were so watered down as to be unrecognizable. She wanted a new job with more independence, and she wanted out of the health care industry.

"My weight and blood pressure are way above normal. I know it's because I am so frustrated," Joanna said. "I can't stand the petty gossip and the endless meetings, so I eat to comfort myself. The problem is, I don't know what else to do."

Making a career change when you're over forty is scary, even more so as you get older. But change is also exciting when you know the small steps that get you where you want to go. "It's possible to do what you love at any age," I said to Joanna. "But first you will have to hold still and look at the past before you move forward. Otherwise you will repeat it."

Holding still was not easy for Joanna, since she's an extrovert. She felt depressed when she was alone too long, and trying to change things in the outside world was her way to solve problems. But setting aside time to summarize the past yielded a rich harvest of understanding for her.

Joanna's autobiography revealed a family pattern of resentment about being controlled and the need to control others. In the family Drama Triangle, her mother played the roles of the Victim and Rescuer, and her father was the Persecutor/Rescuer. As an adult, Joanna played all three roles in her public and private life. Up until a few years ago, she turned to alcohol and drugs when life got difficult, rather than face problems and work through them. She started the process of change by admitting she was an alcoholic and going to Alcoholics Anonymous meetings. "After I stopped drinking, I had to tackle all the issues the booze was blocking," Joanna said, "like my bad temper and getting involved with people I had to take care of."

"You mean with people you *thought* you had to take care of," I said, smiling.

By definition, people in the helping professions take care of people. However, problems arise when caring turns into enabling or rescuing. Doctors, nurses, therapists, ministers, and coaches or mentors have to be careful not to play the role of Rescuer.

"It never occurred to me that I expected to fail," Joanna said after we discussed the Drama Triangle and the life script concepts. "But I can see the logic in that. My father was always angry with his patients for their lack of compliance. He took it personally when they didn't get well. When they died, he would become so enraged that the whole family had to walk on eggshells."

"Some things are beyond our control, Joanna," I said.

She nodded. "That's what I'm starting to see."

The more she stopped trying to control outcomes, the more Joanna realized it was possible to enjoy life, even when people were sick and unhappy. "I see now that others' pain was the trigger," she said. "I didn't want them to suffer. Like a knight on a white horse, I would ride to the rescue, just like my father, and then get mad when they wouldn't change."

This is an example of the societal script I mentioned in chapter 3. This paternal archetype is based on the assumption that people can't take care of themselves, and it persists even though studies show that people who take charge of their health are less likely to get sick and more likely to get well if they do become sick.

To channel Joanna's need to be in control into a positive outlet, I suggested that she get into a business that would use her organizational strength. She said she was interested in being on her own, but she wasn't sure how to transition from public health to a business. Through her research efforts (I cover this process in chapter 7), she found an agency that used both private and government funds to provide home health and nursing care to low-income families. After interviewing with the director and staff, Joanna was hired to administrate the program and raise funds.

Fund-raising is essentially sales, a function that gave Joanna the opportunity to close sales with business people who made contributions to her agency. Selling to decision makers revealed a strength Joanna didn't know she had: the ability to connect with customers. "I never got this kind of acknowledgment before," Joanna said excitedly after she brought in a large contributor. "I enjoy meeting so many different people, but frankly I have problems with my superior. She's moody and manipulative; everyone's afraid of her anger. I am pretty sure she has a drinking problem, but she'll never admit it," Joanna added. "I've been there, so I know how denial works. She also knows she would be hard to replace and that the agency won't let her go because they're afraid she'll sue them. I just want to do my work, but she takes all the fun out of it."

After Joanna had been in the fund-raising job for two and a half years, she was ready to take a bigger risk. She was not blaming (acting as Persecutor toward) her boss, or rescuing coworkers (saying "Let me help you"), or playing Victim (seeing herself as "poor me"). Instead, she focused on solving the problem. "What do you do in your spare time, Joanna?" I asked.

Joanna looked startled; then she said, "Oh, that's easy to answer. On the weekends I get up at 4:30 in the morning and chop wood for my fireplace. Then I organize my house, the garage, and the yard. I'm so good at it that my neighbors are always asking me to help them get their homes in order."

"Why don't you do that for a living?" I asked.

"What?" Joanna said, looking shocked. "You mean be a house-keeper?"

"No, not houses. I mean businesses, shops, banks, parking lots — all those places need to be cleaned."

Joanna was silent. Her mental wheels were spinning. "You're talk-ing about my own janitorial business. I never would have thought of that, but it makes sense. In all my jobs I've been told I'm an expert when it comes to keeping things in order. I just seem to know the efficient way to do anything." (Remember, a strength is so natural that you take it for granted.) "But cleaning. My father, I mean Jack, would have a fit!"

"I'm sure Jack would, but you don't have to tell him what you're doing yet. Wait until you know for sure."

As I said in chapter 2, you'll have enough trouble with your fears, so avoid fearful people during the exploration stage. Parents, relatives, and friends can be well intentioned, but if they are uncomfortable with the unknown, you will only upset them. You can talk with creative peo-ple, however, since they're more comfortable with uncertainty.

"Talk to some people in cleaning companies," I said. "Meet with owners and managers who know the business."

Joanna selected ten janitorial companies of various sizes. Some were large corporations with accounts in high-rise office buildings. Others were medium-sized companies with both large and small accounts. Some owners that she chose to speak to were local entrepreneurs in her town. One was an older man whose janitorial business had an excellent reputation.

After several meetings, Joanna came to see me. She was so excited that words came tumbling out of her mouth. "The cleaning business is

booming, Nancy!" she said. "All the people I talked to were so enthusiastic about the need for quality service. I was even offered a job with
the biggest company in the city. They said they would first have me
work in the field, then train me for management."

I encouraged Joanna to talk with the local man again before she
made her decision: "Let's see what the old pro has to say."

The meeting with the old pro in the cleaning business changed
Joanna's life. Jack (yes, the same name as her father) told Joanna that
he had been looking for a replacement since he would like to retire soon
or work part-time. He suggested that Joanna read articles on the cleaning business and that she think about what they had discussed to make
sure cleaning was what she wanted to do. If she was still interested, Jack
said, he would take her with him and his crew on a typical cleaning
night. This is an example of taking the small steps that lead to success.
Joanna called to give me an update after her field trip with Jack and his
crew. "I like the guy, Nancy. He can be crotchety, but he is good to his
people; some have been with him for years. He said he was sure I could
run the business, but that I would need to learn the efficient way to clean
or I would go broke."

Joanna and Jack had gone to a coffee shop that evening to talk about
how she could ease into the business. After exploring several options,
she decided to work part-time for him in the evenings and part-time at
the agency. "I'm sure that will be okay with my agency," Joanna said.
"I can raise money in the daytime and clean out the banks at night!"

And that is just what Joanna did. One year later (again, small steps),
she quit her fund-raising job and bought the business from Jack, who
stayed on as a consultant while she learned the tricks of the trade. In another year's time she was making twice what she made at the agency,
and she made all the decisions. She called me occasionally to talk about
the ups and downs of entrepreneurship. Some days she felt like giving
up and going back to what she knew (the middle stage of change). I
would always say, "Well, you could go back to agency work. I'm sure
they'd be glad to have you back."

"No way, Nancy," she would say hastily. "Be patient with me, I'm just venting."

And Joanna's father did have a fit when he heard about Joanna's decision to buy the cleaning business. "We didn't raise you to do that kind of work!" Jack shouted over the phone. "What about all that education we paid for, all gone to waste." (Note the Persecutor language.) In the past, Joanna would have believed what Jack said about her, and she would have felt worthless, thus relieving him of any responsibility for his bad behavior. But since her work on her autobiography, she thought of him as Jack, not her father (a powerful word).

"I would never have thought my father was afraid of criticism," Joanna said. "He seems so confident and self-assured. But I know Jack worries about what other people think, particularly his colleagues. He's really quite conventional; he can't stand it when people disapprove of him."

I asked Joanna to send copies of a few bank deposit slips to Jack, with a note about her satisfied customers. "He'll come around when he sees how much money you're making and that your brain is being used to help customers," I said.

And come around Jack did. Now he brags about Joanna to his friends and colleagues: "My daughter, the successful businesswoman."

Joanna was in her early forties when we met, several years before *Work with Passion* was published. Joanna let me use her story in that book and in subsequent editions. She was a favorite with readers, so I asked if I could update her story in this book. "Of course, I would be honored," Joanna said.

Joanna is in her late sixties now, and she is still in the cleaning business. Recently, she sent an email saying that she was tired of managing employees, keeping up with the increasing costs of leasing parking-lot sweepers, and dealing with the customers who complained all the time. I wrote back to say that I thought it was time for Joanna to sell the parking-lot-sweeping business. While she was at it, she could get rid of everything in her life except what she used and loved (as explained in chapter 2). Once the clutter and outdated possessions were out of her life, then she could focus on the part of the business she loved, cleaning down pillows and feather pillows.

I got the idea for a business cleaning down pillows and feather pillows after I read Joanna's description of her pillow-cleaning customers and how appreciative they were of the result, as opposed to her hard-to-please parking-lot-sweeping customers. Even the word *pillow* was in Joanna's email address. "I think the pillow-cleaning business is your niche," I wrote. "It's a match for your values and for your customers' values."

Joanna's parking-lot customers wanted the cheapest and fastest service possible, whereas her pillow-cleaning customers raved about the hygienic, sweet-smelling results, meaning they valued aesthetics and good health, as did Joanna. Remember that her degrees were in the health field. After we exchanged a few more emails, Joanna said she would think about selling the business. In the meantime she went to work eliminating the clutter and debris from her house and outbuildings, making innumerable trips to the dump, she said. Several months later, she sold her parking-lot-cleaning business to a competitor.

Today Joanna revels in the simple life. "Thanks for giving me a push. I should have sold the business a long time ago. But you know how it is: misery was familiar," Joanna said, and we laughed. "I feel as though I'm living in an organized dream." (Do you recall that Joanna's top strength is organization?)

"Downsizing was the answer," Joanna added. "I had no idea how much I would get rid of when I started. Taking small steps is a wise strategy, because that keeps anxiety in check. Even so, in the middle of the process I got so sick I had to go to the hospital. It was a nasty virus, but I also know it was my fear of the unknown acting up, as you warned me it would."

Joanna said she was learning new ways to expand her pillow-cleaning business. "A few of my younger employees are helping me to build a website. I've learned so much from them about computers. When I said pillows need to be cleaned or replaced once a year, they said I needed to highlight that information on the first page of the website.

"I just love working with the millennium generation," Joanna said excitedly. "They are good kids, so bright and creative. After all, they were brought up by boomer parents."

Even with all the positive changes she was making, Joanna said she knew better than to get complacent. "I have to keep a watchful eye on my script, even at my age," Joanna said. "I know the moment I start thinking irrationally I'll go backward." Staying on top of old habits of thinking is a lifelong effort. Especially during times of upheaval and change, we are likely to go back to what is familiar, like skiers who revert to the snowplow stance when they get in trouble on the slopes. But each time Joanna resisted the pull of the past, her faith in a better future grew stronger.

Writing Goals

Goals need to be written down so your subconscious will accept what you say as logical. For example, say your goal is to be in a committed relationship, but you're afraid you'll make the wrong choice, you'll lose your freedom, or you or the other person will exit when conflict arises, since this is what happened to you before. Your subconscious knows you're not ready for a committed relationship. What you need is a better relationship with yourself. Here's the sentence that will convince your subconscious your goal is logical: "I love and accept myself exactly as I am." This means that you accept failures as well as successes, your age, appearance, personality, and temperament.

Next, write this goal: "I have firm boundaries." These words instruct your subconscious that setting limits is characteristic of healthy relationships. To lock in this concept, write: "I am balanced between my needs and the needs of others."

What else do you need in order to be ready for a committed relationship? How about this goal: "I am honest and direct." Being honest and direct is another logical choice, even if this means you have a "clear the air" fight with someone. Remember what Bill Parcells said: you have to be honest with people if you want to be effective.

Finally, write: "I am ready for a committed, mutually respectful relationship."

Note the order of the goals and how the words you use prepare you for success. As an example, the word *ready* addresses the need to complete what is on your plate — an obligation, a project, or some unfinished business from the past. The words *mutually respectful* acknowledge the respect *you* will feel for your new partner, as well as that person's respect for you.

For an example of how to set the small goals that lead to greater success, or, as Bill Parcells says, making the down you are in, write your goals in the following order:

1. I love and accept myself exactly as I am.
2. I have firm boundaries.
3. I am balanced between my needs and the needs of others.
4. I am honest and direct.
5. I am ready for a committed, mutually respectful relationship.

These sentences are like an architect's blueprint. The "house" is not built yet, but the design is there for your subconscious to follow. Read or repeat the sentences out loud in the morning, at noon, and before you go to sleep. In time, you'll see signs of change.

For example, after you affirm "I love and accept myself exactly as I am" for a few weeks, mistakes don't upset you the way they used to do. You admit and correct errors and then move on, because you accept yourself even when you make mistakes.

If you're an introvert, you notice that you're becoming more comfortable with being alone. Equally important, you're comfortable with letting extroverts be around others. As an extrovert, you are comfortable with being active and outgoing, as well as comfortable with introverts, who prefer quiet, intimate gatherings.

Once you start repeating "I am honest and direct" on a regular basis, you say what you think without waffling and avoiding. You're also more open to hearing other points of view, even if they are at odds with your beliefs.

You'll know your subconscious has accepted firm boundaries as logical when you can say no without feeling guilty and yes to what makes sense. Others accept your new boundaries too, an example of "as within so without." This concept means that when your thinking shifts, the outer world shifts to reflect your new perspective.

Once your choices consistently demonstrate self-acceptance, firm boundaries, balance between your needs and the needs of others, and honest, direct communication, it's only logical that you'll also attract a partner who is well balanced.

Paul Changes His Script

Paul was an executive in a large financial institution. He wanted to keep working past retirement age, but he wasn't sure what he wanted to do. "I struggle to go to work everyday," Paul said to me in our first session. "I'm so frustrated that I'm thinking about taking early retirement. Before I leave I'd like to know what I want to do next."

Professionally Paul did well, except when he reported to bosses who wouldn't give him credit for his leadership ability. Rather than repeat that experience with future bosses, Paul asked for help with his career transition.

"How do you feel about sales?" I asked Paul.

"Sales? Me? No way. I don't like to pressure people," Paul said, looking uncomfortable.

"The best salespeople are educators," I said. "As an example, think of the people who want financial stability. You can show them how to achieve that goal."

"Oh, I see. Since I understand what it takes to be financially stable, I could sell that service."

"Yes, exactly right. You have what your customer needs. You don't have to pressure them; just show them what you know."

"But that's so simple," Paul said, looking surprised.

"I know," I said, and then we laughed.

To make sure I was on track, I asked Paul if he would like to meet two of my clients who were in sales. One was an extrovert, the other more of an introvert. "After they meet with you, I'll ask them what they think of you, and you can tell me what you think of them," I said.

"Okay, I would like that," Paul said.

My clients said they thought Paul would be a natural at sales. He just needed to know what he wanted to sell. "He is so knowledge-able about financial matters," my introverted client said. "I learned a great deal just listening to him. He doesn't know how marketable he is. He just needs to meet with some people so he'll have something to compare himself with, like you suggested that I do. He was glad to know that being an introvert is an advantage, since we think deeply about matters."

My extroverted client agreed that Paul was misplaced in a staff position, that he would excel in a line position, meaning he would be in direct contact with customers. "He is very humble, considering his accomplishments. Connecting with customers will give Paul what he's missing in a staff job. I know they'll like and trust him. I would certainly buy from him." This client said he'd asked Paul to stay in touch with him. "We're going to meet again after he talks with sales managers and CFOs in his field."

Paul was impressed with both of my clients. "I have a different picture of sales after talking with the men you referred me to," he said. "Both men said sales is educating people. I do that all the time with my team members and the people above me. I just didn't think that what I do is selling," he added. "People have always said I'm a good mentor; they always want to come to my meetings. Talking with your clients gave me an appreciation for that skill. I guess I took what I do for granted."

Like all my clients who are in midlife and beyond, Paul was relieved to discover that he knew enough to succeed at what he wanted to do. "Your clients said you've got to believe in what you're selling if you want customers to trust you," Paul said. "Otherwise, they won't buy from you. That explains why salespeople made a bad impression on me. They didn't believe in what they were doing; they were in it for the money."

After meeting with sales managers, chief financial officers, and bank managers, Paul met with the director of a company that provided investment services for high-income clients. Since he'd grown up with wealth, Paul felt at ease with wealthy people. In fact, he said he'd already made his first sales. "Two of the sales managers I met with asked for my advice on money management. One just came into a large inheritance, and the other wants to invest in income-producing properties."

Without knowing it, Paul had sold himself in the process of interviewing salespeople! He was surprised that people felt so comfortable talking with him about money and property. This made him think that he could eventually have his own financial planning practice, after he had worked for a few years with an investment firm. That wouldn't have occurred to him had he not changed the way he thought about salespeople. Illogical thinking had kept Paul stuck in the past because he'd assumed it was his lot in life to report to bosses who didn't know as much as he did. Recognizing that he would do his best in the authority role put Paul in the niche where he belonged.

Paul's story is an example of passion in midlife and beyond not being what you expect. In fact, it's better than anything you can imagine. So just keep working the process and let the outcome surprise you.

The three criteria for setting realistic goals are measurement, motivation, and responsibility, which I discuss in the following sections. As you will see, goals that you failed to reach in the past were unrealistic because they were too vague, they weren't what you truly wanted to do, or there were too many variables you couldn't control. The goals you

did reach were precise and fueled by genuine enthusiasm, and you and
you alone were responsible for the outcome.

Measurement

Successful companies set measurable goals. At the same time, they adapt
to changes in the marketplace. Sales managers cannot sell products or
services unless they measure the market, the competition, and the
sales team's capabilities. For example, your goal is to make more
money. How much money do you want, when do you need it, and why?
There are two ways to increase income: you can cut your overhead
or increase your productivity or both. Thus, the goal "more money"
can be measured as follows: "I will cut my expenses in the areas of
_____ by \$_____a month. To increase
my income by \$_____, I will provide the following services." Then
write about what you will do and for whom.

    You may also need to get rid of time-consuming habits like brows-
ing the Internet or talking on the phone. If so, include a statement like,
"I am efficient; I make good use of my time."

    As you write, you may realize that efficiency is what you need, since
you tend to waste time on distractions. If this is the case, first write a
paragraph about what efficiency means to you, and what causes you to
go off on tangents (fear of criticism, poverty, old habits, and so on).
Then write your money goal. In other words, make efficiency your priority, and then you will make "more money."

Internal Motivation

Once you measure a goal, ask why you want the goal. Any goal has to
be internally motivated or you won't sustain the effort it takes to get
there. Even if you do reach it, you won't be satisfied, because the goal
is not authentic.

    Remember John Holt, the innovative educator I mentioned in chap-
ter 3? He said that doing tasks for internal reasons increases learning.

Before you set a goal, ask, "What will I learn from the process of getting to this goal? Do I just want the reward?"

Joanna decided at a young age to follow in her father's footsteps, which saved her the struggle that goes with figuring out one's own path in life. She jumped through academic hoops and got high marks and two advanced degrees. Then she moved steadily up the ladder of nonprofit institutions. She made plenty of money and had status, but she wasn't happy. To cope with her frustration, she overate, drank, and used drugs, until she decided to put fulfillment before money and prestige.

Bill Parcells assumes that players love football, because otherwise they wouldn't be on the field. As he says, if you aren't motivated to do the work, you don't belong on the team — or in any job for that matter. Self-correction is a sign that players' hearts are in what they're doing.

The key to internal motivation is your interest in what you're learning. You can't fake interest or the lack of it. You're eager to learn more about what interests you; what you couldn't care less about doesn't interest you, which is why you can't get motivated to do it.

Think of a time when your interest pushed through your fears. Where were you and what were you doing? Now think of a time when you were not interested, when you were just going through the motions. Because you were externally motivated, you failed. You can't fail when your goals are authentic. Simple as it seems, success is the result of doing what interests you, as was the case with Paul. And if the process fascinates you, the outcome is the frosting on the cake. The best incentive is having a goal that has meaning for you.

Personal Responsibility

Now that your goal is measurable and internally motivated, the next criterion is that you're responsible for the achievement of the goal. When the end result depends on others or circumstances beyond your control, the likelihood of success decreases, since you can't be responsible for what people do or don't do, or events that were set in motion a long time ago. For example, you can't be responsible for a goal that says, "I want a promotion in six months." This goal is measurable and internally motivated, but you need the help of other people or events to attain the goal — a supervisor or revenue growth in the company. But you can be responsible for the goal if you write it as follows: "I improve my productivity, knowledge, and performance so that I am qualified for a promotion. In the meantime, I explore options outside my company that will pay me for the increased value of my performance."

While researching options outside his company, Paul realized he was a natural at helping others with money and property, a strength he took for granted. Fortunately, Paul seized opportunity when it appeared on his doorstep.

Measure your dreams; be sure they're internally motivated and that you and you alone are responsible for the outcome. Then you're ready to write a six-month must-have list, following the "set and reach small goals" philosophy.

A Six-Month Must-Have List

Why six months, you may ask? Why not a year, or five years? Setting goals in a short time span follows Parcells's third rule of leadership: set and reach small goals. Setting longer-term goals does not work as well, because then achievement is such a long way off. Not only that, if you're changing and growing, by the time you reach your long-term goals they may no longer be what you want.

Start by circling a date on your calendar six months from now. Then make a list of what you *know* you can achieve by that date. Write down everything you can think of: a new hairstyle, wardrobe, friends, job, or business, or the completion of a project. You'll probably write the list several times before it feels right.

Let the list sit overnight, then read it again. Are these must-haves or merely cravings? If in the meanwhile you've thought of other needs, like confidence or peace of mind, put those goals on the list too. Now reduce your list to five must-haves. Write a paragraph describing each goal in the present tense, as if you already have it.

Let's say one of your goals is to lose weight. Just as you did when you asked why you didn't already have a committed relationship, ask why you are overweight — what fear is at the root of the problem? This question puts weight in the symptom category, not the cause category. Do you use food to avoid painful feelings, such as anger, anxiety, or frustration? Do you have a negative attitude toward your body and sexuality? Is food a substitute for sexual pleasure? Are your attitudes toward food similar to those of your parents or other relatives?

When painful feelings come up, stop and experience the feelings *before* you eat. Once you've felt the feeling all the way to the end, then you can eat. If you do this every time you experience painful feelings, you'll discover that these feelings pass and are replaced by other feelings. It also helps to exercise and meditate frequently while breathing deeply to help move the feelings through the body. A sense of humor will keep any tendency to dramatize the situation in check, so rent funny movies and read books that make you laugh out loud. In time, you'll see that unpleasant feelings are not permanent and that they're part of a fully lived life; maturity gives you the courage to experience them. Like an accomplished actor, you'll get more and more adept at recognizing and expressing *all* your emotions. Then eating will assume its normal place in your life.

Again, a goal has to be internally motivated or you won't do what it takes to reach the goal. If you truly want to be smaller, don't say, "I need to eat less or I need to exercise more." That is what you need to do, but you won't do it as long as you use food to numb the feelings. To feel comfortable with being at the right weight for you, write down the amount you know you can lose in six months. Be practical. As Parcells said, set and reach small goals, since this gets you in the habit of winning. Setting unrealistic goals only fuels the habit of failure. In other words, emulate successful people.

Weight loss experts agree that losing several pounds a month is a realistic goal. Gradual weight loss gives your subconscious mind time to accept and adjust to the slimmer you, resetting your self-image software, so to speak. The subconscious also has to believe that you'll face up to the problem that overeating is masking. Here's an example of a six-month weight-loss goal you can reach: "I face and solve my problems. I feel all my feelings, since that's how I know I'm alive. I am comfortable weighing what is normal for my body size and bone structure. I exercise four or five times a week, and I eat nourishing food. I like how I feel and look."

Note that this goal is measurable and internally motivated, and that you and you alone are responsible for getting there. Now the "law" of interest goes to work for you. This law draws information to you seemingly from out of nowhere. After you write down your goal about weight, for example, you notice articles and books on problem solving, weight loss, and nutrition. You overhear conversations that capture your attention; you see experts on television discussing weight and health. You ask healthy, fit people how they got that way, and then you copy their example.

As you repeat your affirmation, you notice that your body is doing the eating, not your emotions. You may hire a trainer to help you stay on track; you may join a gym or a walking group or exercise on your own.

Now you're in the second stage of change, maintaining healthy habits. But watch out, the failure script doesn't give up easily. When a relapse occurs, stop and think about what or who triggered the setback. Did you have a discouraging encounter with someone? Did one of the six basic fears cause the relapse? If so, face up to the problem and then get back on track.

It may take longer than six months to get to your normal weight, so affirm only the weight you know you can lose in six months. Once you reach that goal, you can write a weight loss goal for the next six months.

Some goals take longer to reach than others. Getting rid of distractions is harder than buying a new wardrobe, for example. Don't be surprised when a goal drops off the list. Just affirm what you really need. Here's how to write a distilled must-have list:

1. I am open to change and growth.
2. I am comfortable weighing _____ pounds; I like how I look.
3. I take good care of myself.
4. I am comfortable getting paid to do what comes naturally.
5. I enjoy and live in the present moment.

Do you see why you use the word *comfortable* when you talk about your weight and making money? This word encourages the subconscious mind to let go of what's comfortable now: not getting paid what you're worth and being overweight. As you affirm your comfort with having a trim, fit body and getting paid what you deserve, soon you'll feel the inner click that lets you know the unconscious has accepted these goals as logical.

Note that all the must-haves on this list follow the three guidelines for success. They are internally motivated, they are measurable, and you are responsible for the achievement of the goals.

Starting a creative project is the same as any goal: break the goal down into small steps. What do you need to do first? Then write a goal that addresses that need. For example, you want to write or paint or sculpt, but you lack self-discipline, the ability to stick to the task until it represents your best effort. Your first goal needs to be "I am comfortable with being self-disciplined. I enjoy the process of getting there."

To repeat: you're happy when you get what you expect, and every choice changes you, so make sure your expectations and actions are in line with reality. When in doubt, work with experts in the field who can show you what it takes to get where you want to go. A good rule of thumb is, if you're still enjoying the process after a year's effort, you're on the passion track.

As you grow in your craft, you'll naturally expand what you know. The key is to fold this new activity into your life gradually, not taking on more than you can do well. Let your new dream come true in small steps, just as your previous dreams became reality. Be assured, if you're willing to do the work that being the best requires, you'll succeed.

The Collage

Now that you've written your six-month must-have list, you're ready to make a collage, a visual representation of your goals. First, go to an art supply store and buy a glue stick and a sheet of poster board in a color that appeals to you. Next, cut pictures out of magazines, catalogs, or other publications. These images can be beautiful scenery, clothing, children, food, travel, or people you identify with — whatever captures your imagination. You can also use favorite photographs. If you are drawn to sentences in ads or articles, cut those out and place them with your pictures.

Once you've assembled the pictures and sayings, arrange them on the poster board. Let your first arrangement sit overnight. The next day rearrange the collage as needed until it feels just right; then glue the images and words to the poster board. If you prefer, you can use digital images from the Internet for this project, putting them together in a collage that you print from your computer.

The collage is like dessert, a sweet end to the meat-and-potatoes work of the previous chapters. Viewing the completed collage will be a gestalt experience, since you'll be looking at your authentic self's deepest desires. As with a dream, images in the collage may be symbolic for you. A bird with bright yellow plumage sitting high on the branch of a tree is a lovely sight to behold, but it may symbolize your need for freedom and your hope for the future. Similarly, pictures of happy couples may indicate a loving bond with your partner, or may tell you that this is what you need. Images of men and women can also mean you need to balance the active and receptive aspects of your personality, to pay attention to your feelings and intuition as well as to your thoughts and senses. Calm, peaceful pictures indicate the need for retreat and contemplation. Hot, bright images say you're ready to take action.

If the images in the collage indicate goals not on your written list, the collage is the more accurate source of information. For example, say your written list describes social and travel goals, to the exclusion of alone time. But the colors in the collage are cool, and the images are of nature and of individuals walking on a beach or sitting alone with a book — and no cities or groups. In this case, your authentic self wants time to reflect. Rewrite your must-have list to match the images in the collage, since these are what you need. You can always make a new collage six months from now, when you're ready to socialize and travel.

Some of the images and words that make it into your collage will surprise you, as will the collage when you look at it six months from now. "Oh, *that's* what that means," you'll think.

A Sample Collage

You read about Mike, the salesman who eventually accepted that he was at his best in a start-up and writing about sales. Not all my clients wind up working for themselves or writing books, but they all want to be more creative and independent, although they may not know that when we meet. All they know is that they're so frustrated with what they're doing that they'll do whatever it takes to change.

Mike was frustrated because he was trying to be too extroverted, spreading himself too thin instead of focusing. He was not aware that he was a growth type, meaning he liked to start things and then start something new when he was done. The need for new projects is typical of creative people, whether they are entrepreneurs, independent contractors, or artists. If you want to torture these people, make them do the same thing over and over again.

However, impatience with the slowness of change was Mike's downfall, since he was used to making things happen. He felt discouraged about how long he was taking to find his correct niche, until I assured him that he was right on schedule. Change does not always have to be a ride on a slow freight train. Sometimes you leap to higher levels of understanding, as Mike did while speaking on the phone with his brother. As usual, the brother had a long list of complaints, the same complaints he'd had for years. In the past Mike would have offered solutions and then gotten angry when his brother countered with "Yes, but..."

"This time I just listened, and then I changed the subject," Mike said. "It felt strange to not be angry. My mind was peaceful. I think this is what you've been trying to tell me, but I had to experience detachment to understand how powerful it is."

The images in Mike's collage confirmed his needs, telling him that he needed to pare life down to essentials and not take himself too seriously. Your collage will do something similar for you. Here is how Mike described his collage:

> The picture in the center is home, the place where my wife and I come to recharge, relax, enjoy. It's our paradise. Starting clockwise with the dog picture at the top, this is a reminder to have fun and not take myself too seriously. But I still need time for quiet reflection, which is represented by the mountain and still lake to the right of the dog.
>
> The animal pictures represent our pets, which give us joy. The man enjoying himself at the piano represents the creative part of me, the desire to learn something that I don't currently do and my desire to set the longtime goal of learning to play the piano.
>
> The next picture represents the beauty and peace I find in nature. The stone image in a museum represents art and culture — which are important to me, something I want more of. The next picture is of friends and family and reminds me of the joy and richness that both bring. The boat picture represents global travel, a desire to understand other cultures outside the United States.
>
> Finally, the rowing picture represents my goal to work with people who pull together. Should my business reach that level, that's the way I want my company to work, even if the company is

just myself. I guess you could say the picture shows that I'm undivided, not pulling against myself as I did in the past.

On the whole, I feel a sense of accomplishment when I look at this collage. It gives me something to aim for and a chance to reflect on how I'm doing. It just struck me that the work aspect of the collage is in the perfect proportion. I think this shows that I believe the other aspects of my life are as important as what I do professionally.

A by-product of Mike's work on himself was the positive effect it had on his marriage. I had worked with his wife several years before Mike called me. Now they both do what makes them happy.

SUMMARY

1. Set small goals.
2. Measure your goal.
3. Make sure the goal is internally motivated.
4. Be responsible for reaching the goal.
5. Make a collage to visualize goals.

CHAPTER 7

Find Your Perfect Niche

O brave new world, that has such people in it!
— MIRANDA, IN SHAKESPEARE'S *THE TEMPEST*

Now comes the payoff for all the hard work you did in the previous chapters: finding your perfect niche in work. You'll have fun with this part of the process because you're prepared. And now that you know who you are and what you value, you'll find the people who need your strengths to solve their problems. In fact, you may already know these people.

Many times, my clients discover they have contacts right in their backyards. They're relieved to know they don't have to scour the Internet, go to dozens of networking groups, move across the country, or use conventional job-hunting techniques to find the right niche. On the contrary, the process of interviewing starts with people they already know and then widens to include people that those people know, and so on, until they reach their target audience.

As you've discovered from reading the stories in this book, the passion search is intuitive, not linear, yet it always winds up in exactly the right place. Many of my clients say, after they're in their perfect niches, "But this is so obvious; why didn't I see it before?" If, like them, you've done the work outlined in the previous chapters, then this chapter will guide you to your niche. Again, don't lose heart when you run into roadblocks. This means you're "pushing the river": you need more preparation, or you're returning to the past. When this happens, step back and examine your motives. Ask yourself if the false self's vanity pushed you into doing what your authentic self does not want to do.

Know Your Personality Type

Before you set up meetings with people doing the work that interests you, make sure you know your personality type — whether you're a partner, team, or solo type, an introvert or an extrovert. I can't emphasize strongly enough the importance of knowing yourself. Misunderstanding, conflict, and failure are the inevitable results of trying to force closeness with people who aren't compatible. For example, if you value independence, you'll be at odds with people who value security. Similarly, if you're an introvert, you'll feel exhausted if you spend too much time with action-loving extroverts. If you're an extrovert, you'll feel frustrated around quiet, slow-paced introverts.

The following three personality types are not mutually exclusive; as with temperament, some traits show up in more than one type. But one type indicates your optimal way of relating to others at home and work.

The Partner Type

Are you at your best when you interact with one other person? Do you like to say and hear, "What do you think?" If so, you're a partner type. Your partner can be a partner in business, an agent, a coach, or client. The key is that your interaction with this person is one-on-one. Here are more characteristics of your personality type:

- You need to be alone about half the time.
- Productivity increases when you work with your partner.
- You are self-reliant (paradoxical, but true).
- You are a good listener.
- You are motivated by praise from your partner.

Other clues that you're the partner type: You always had one close friend, even in childhood. You're happiest when paired, in romance, sports, at dinner. You are fascinated by duos; famous teams intrigue you. You'd like to be part of one yourself.

The Team Type

If you're the team type of personality, you feel at home in a group, at work, in clubs, on social networking sites, or as a member of political and charitable organizations. Here are more traits that define your team personality:

- You need to be alone about 20 percent of the time.
- You take a consensus approach to problem solving.
- You're gregarious and outgoing.
- Productivity increases around teammates.
- You're motivated by praise from your team.

Other clues that you're a team type: You grew up in a large family, you had many friends throughout your school years and you still have many friendships, and your contact base is getting larger with time. You love team sports, and you'd like to be a member of an outstanding team.

The Solo Type

If you like to look at an end result and say "I did that," you're a solo. That can be the operation you perform, the company you build, the sale you make, the project you create from scratch, or the house you remodel. Here are more traits that describe your personality:

- You need to be alone 60–70 percent of the time.
- Productivity increases when you work by yourself.
- You have a few close friends.
- Time to think is your number one priority.
- Pleasing yourself motivates you.

Other clues that you're a solo type: You have a vivid imagination; you always entertained yourself as a child. You made your own money early. Others have always followed your lead, although you aren't interested in leading others. You see yourself as distinct but not separate from others.

How you manage stress also reveals your personality type and temperament. For example, if you retreat to regain balance, you're a solo (introvert). As a partner, you talk things over with your partner (a mixture of introvert and extrovert). If you reduce stress by talking with many people, you are the team type (extrovert).

Solos work well with teams as long as they can remain in an autonomous role, either as a consultant or contractor. Solos also do well in partnerships when the partner is another solo. The partner type can feel comfortable with a group as long as it's small. Team types do best around other team types. Since they thrive on stimulation, they feel lonely and bored around partners and solos.

Now that you know your personality type and your temperament, you're ready to find the people who have your values and who are compatible with your type and temperament. If they have problems you can and want to solve, then this is the niche where you will grow to your full potential and make the money you need (need, not crave).

The Right Niche

Back in the 1970s, Michael Phillips, a former banker and the author of *The Seven Laws of Money*, said that the first law of money is to do what you love and the money will follow: "Right livelihood is a concept that places money secondary to what you are doing. It's something like a steam engine, where the engine, fire and water working together create steam for forward motion. Money is like steam; it comes from the interaction of fire (passion) and water (persistence) brought together in the right circumstance, the engine."[1] Phillips says two factors characterize right livelihood. One, you can do the work for a long time, meaning years or even a lifetime. Longevity is necessary so that the work can change you into a better person. Two, the work is good for you and also good for society (passion clue #3).

When you're in the right niche, you don't want to be anywhere other than where you are. Nor do you compare yourself with others. You're content because you know you're making a contribution to society that is important to you (values again). Whether you're a handyman, a nurse, the president of a company, a small business owner, or a chef, the work makes you over as you are doing it. This means you learn from mistakes, changing what needs to be changed until you succeed, which changes you into a better, more effective person. At the same time your growth is having a positive effect on those you serve.

The perfect niche can be what you're already doing, but perhaps you need to reshape it to fit new circumstances, as Joanna did with her cleaning business. At one time, running her parking-lot-sweeping business was rewarding emotionally and financially. But as time went by, her feelings about her competition, her demanding customers, and her age were signs she needed to focus on what she loved: her pillow-cleaning business and working as an independent consultant to the new owners of her business.

Sometimes the perfect niche is a new position in the same company or a different boss. You may go to work for a smaller company, or, as you will see in Mike's case, you may join forces with partners to create a cutting-edge marketing business.

Whatever you do, start by choosing the work that challenges you, since challenge is how you reach your full potential. Doing what you already know causes you to stagnate and lose touch with the times. Don't start with what will change the world. Trying to improve the world can be a way to avoid what needs improving in your life. This was the case with one of my clients, who said he wanted to help the world.

"What part of the world are you referring to?" I asked Bob. "Do you want to help your neighborhood, your city, another country, what?"

"None of those, I just, you know, want to help the world," Bob said.

"No, I don't know," I replied. "You have to be specific."

We didn't get very far in our session that day until I walked with Bob to where his car was parked in my driveway. I was shocked by the car's appearance; it was a mess inside and out. "If you want to help the world, Bob, I suggest you start with your car," I said, gesturing toward his vehicle.

Bob looked at his car, back at me, and blinked a couple of times, and then he started laughing.

"Don't hold back, Nancy," he said, and we both laughed.

The next time I met with Bob, he said he'd decided to clean up his life before he took on the messes in the world, starting with going to Alcoholics Anonymous meetings, which I had suggested he do before we went any further. After Bob got sober, he subcontracted his carpentry services to contractors who remodeled run-down houses. Today, Bob concentrates on what he needs to change about himself, which, ironically, improves Bob's world and the world at large.

The Entrepreneurial Trend

The entrepreneurial trend in business has expanded exponentially since I began my work in 1976. This is largely due to your generation's venturesome spirit; to explosive growth in technology, the Internet, and service businesses; and to women's influence in the marketplace. In fact, many women were the first to start home-based businesses, now a popular and efficient way to work.

Women do well in their own businesses because they're comfortable with starting small. They aren't afraid to take risks that others consider foolish, as Joanna did when she walked away from a high-paying job and disregarded her father's disapproval.

Women are also less likely to need the ego boost that comes from appearances: big offices, job titles, high-powered associates, and large incomes. And they're less prone than men to sacrifice emotional needs for money and status. All that testosterone can be a disadvantage! Also, admitting mistakes is easier for most women, as is asking for help, a result of having humility, which forges lasting bonds with customers and clients. For both men and women, climbing the corporate ladder is not the ideal it was in past decades, thanks to the banditlike behavior of some chief executive officers, particularly in the financial arena.

If you're bored with endless meetings and slow decision-making, you may be an entrepreneur in the making. At the very least you'll do better in a smaller organization, where turnaround time is shorter. Another sign that you're in the wrong niche is that you want to be doing rather than talking about doing.

Entrepreneurs and owners of businesses are not always the same person. Serial entrepreneurs like to get things up and running and then move on to other businesses, whereas business owners can stay with the same businesses for a long time. What follows is a list of traits that describe both serial entrepreneurs and business owners. If most of the items describe you, then your niche is a business or series of businesses, a solo practice, or creative projects of your own design.

- You are self-disciplined.
- You manage money well.
- What you say matches what you do.
- You trust your instincts.
- You drop what is not working.
- Growth is more important than your ego.
- You will live in a tent if that's what it takes to survive.
- The start-up phase fascinates you.
- You're always thinking of ways to improve.
- A satisfied customer makes your day.

In addition, the business, solo practice, or creative project you choose has to be a match for your values and temperament, or you'll fail. But failure is the way your authentic self gets you to where you will succeed, even if you have to be dragged kicking and screaming into the right niche.

When your attempts don't work out, don't spend time with regret and recrimination. Regroup, recoup your losses, and try again until what you do is an exact match for your strengths, values, needs, and temperament. Then you can't fail.

Using the "Yellow Pages"

By now you may know what you want to do. But if you need more help, the rest of this chapter will give you tips on how to do research, contact people, hold low-pressure meetings with decision makers, write effective résumés and proposals, set hourly or daily fees, and negotiate offers that are fair to both parties. The same process applies whether your goal is to have your own business, a solo practice, or a creative project.

Since the diamonds you seek may be buried in your backyard, begin by looking at the index section in your local "Yellow Pages." This is the part of the phone book where work categories are listed from A to Z. You can also look at categories of work that aren't in the phone book by Googling websites that interest you.

Open your phone book to the index section of the "Yellow Pages." Go through the list of work categories slowly, making note of any category that interests you. Since this exercise can be mentally taxing, try doing it in three sittings, going from A to G, then H to M, and then N to Z.

You can also consider hobbies that interest you, since what you do for recreation can be passion clues. Remember that passion is what you value for yourself *and* for others, as when you read a good book and you want everyone else to read it, whereas a hobby is just for your pleasure. As an example, if you love to cook and you also want everyone else to eat what you cook, you'd enjoy either working as a chef in a restaurant or creating specialty food products that you place in grocery stores, such as breads and muffins that promote your name, as one of my clients did.

If you love to ride bicycles and you think everyone else should use this green form of transportation, you'd be happy selling or repairing bikes, especially now that manufacturers are targeting riders of all ages and those who commute as well as those who ride their bikes to shopping centers. One of my clients took a two-week workshop to learn how to repair bikes. With his certification, Eric was able to get a job in any bike shop.

When you're done with the index section, you'll have about thirty categories on your master list. Let this list sit overnight. Then break the list down to fifteen interests. Next, narrow that list down to five categories of interest, and jot down the page numbers where those entities are located.

Ask yourself whether any of these categories are hobbies, what you want to do just for you. If some are personal interests, then cross those off the list. Some categories will be what you're already doing, as was the case for Bob, the carpenter.

Bob had remodeling houses on his list of interests, but he thought being a carpenter didn't help the world, so he rejected it. The origin of this illogical conclusion was Bob's admiration for his minister father, an extrovert who emphasized service to others and who rarely took time for himself or his family. Not surprisingly, Bob concluded at an early age that saving the world was more important than he was, and this led to his "I can't be happy if the world is not happy" script. As he wrote his life story, he realized that his father's motives were not as authentic as they had appeared to be when Bob was a boy. In reality, Ralph, the father, was a distant man who used the ministry to avoid intimacy, just as Bob used alcohol to avoid his feelings.

Looking at Ralph with grown-up eyes helped Bob to accept that carpentry was the right niche for his personality type and temperament, and that, in fact, Ralph, too, was probably an introvert, but Ralph had tried to be what he thought others wanted him to be. To succeed, Bob just needed to stop drinking and trying to save the world.

As soon as you select your top five categories, the law of interest will go to work for you. You may remember a time when you wanted to purchase a certain item and then you noticed it everywhere. Once you identify a specific interest, you find examples of it everywhere, which is how Bob found the contractor who remodeled run-down houses. While driving around one day, he saw the man's truck, the same kind of truck Bob had, so he stopped and introduced himself to the contractor. The next week Bob's truck was parked alongside the contractor's.

Look around you. Everything you see is the result of your interest: your computer, the chair you're sitting on, what you're wearing, even your copy of *Work with Passion in Midlife and Beyond*. Did you go through an elimination process before you bought these items? Did the shopping expedition eventually lead to a decision?

Choosing your right livelihood is also a shopping expedition. You say to yourself, "Not that, not that, not that," until all that remains is what you'd do even when nobody paid you to do it. Most likely, you're already doing what you love; you just can't imagine who would pay you for it (strengths are so natural, remember?).

The Right Niche Is Profitable

Since a job, business, practice, or creative project is not a charity or a hobby, the right niche makes a profit. What you do needs to be what *customers* perceive to have value.

Mark Helow and Jim Schleckser, respectively the founder and the president of the CEO Project, say that a good business has three elements.

1. Demand exists — or you can create demand — that consistently exceeds supply. It helps to have a product that customers love, has recurring revenue and is a non-discretionary purchase.
2. You have a sustainable advantage that is difficult to duplicate. With this advantage often comes unique vertical knowledge, which *deepens over time* [my italics].
3. The economic characteristics (gross margin, return on invested capital, etc.) are favorable.[2]

Helow and Schleckser coach chief executive officers to help them grow their businesses. Both men say that the following CEO actions separate the winners from losers:

Picking the right business/profit model
Putting "A" players in key positions
Implementing "A" processes in customer service and sales[3]

Success in a business, then, begins with a good business model. Then you need to find "A" players to help you succeed; this is true whether you work alone, with a partner, or with a team. According to Helow and Schleckser, "An 'A' player regularly excels and goes beyond expectations, reinvents and improves new situations and is a shining example for others and forwards company values. Ask the question: If you could hire anyone in the world to do this job, would it be that person? If the answer is no, then the person is likely not an 'A.' "[4] Helow and Schleckser say that CEOs often think they hire "A" players when the people are really "B" players, people who meet expectations but do not exceed them. "C" players, they say, do not meet expectations, nor are they examples to others.

To help you imagine the place where you'll exceed your own and others' expectations, try this exercise. First, get into a comfortable position, close your eyes, and breathe deeply. In your mind's eye, envision a flight of stairs that leads down to a beautiful path in the woods. Go down each step slowly, taking time to adapt to your surroundings.

When you reach the bottom, walk down the path until you see a door. On this door is a shiny plaque with your name and a description of your right livelihood — what you do for you and for others.

Open the door and walk in. Where are you? Are you indoors or outdoors? Are you alone or are others there? Is your workplace a home office, a conventional office, a stage, a movie or television set, a building site? Is your car parked nearby, waiting for you to drive to customer locations? Or are you at the airport ready to catch a flight?

What do you do in this place, and who pays you to do it? Are these people your customers, clients, or managers, or do you have a contract or grant? Notice the view and the surroundings. Memorize this place. Enjoy the comfort you feel. Now turn and go back to the door, but before you walk through, look up over the door. There you'll see the amount of money you make each year. Make note of this amount.

Close the door behind you; then walk back down the path and up the stairs, taking each step slowly. When you open your eyes, notice how you feel. Did your imaginary niche match the images in your collage and the must-haves on your written list? Are you surprised by your vision of the future?

If you want to alter your niche, go back down the steps and rearrange things. Keep in mind, though, that first impressions are usually the most accurate. It may take time for this niche to materialize, but leave how-to-make-it-happen up to your subconscious.

Now look at the list of your five categories of interest. Turn to the pages in the phone book where each category is listed. Pick out five companies in each category. Or go online to pick out websites that match your categories. You'll have twenty-five companies of different sizes. As an example, here are Mike's categories of interest:

1. Consultants, sales — p. 139
2. Management consultants — p. 453

It's easy to see what interests Mike. When he first designed his sales consulting business, he thought he had to market himself as a big company to impress prospective clients. Being a solo operator lacked status and prestige. So he wrote his own sales training manual, which was similar to those he used when he was a salesperson in large consulting firms. Even the first draft of his manual was full of corporate jargon. He got nowhere.

The breakthrough came when Mike realized he'd used corporate jargon to mask his fear that he wasn't good enough on his own to land sales training contracts. And he was right, since large companies tend to favor established consulting firms with large staffs. But the roadblock was Mike's lack of interest in working with corporations. His authentic self wanted to help individuals become better salespeople — to use his strengths to help them succeed — so he went back to the drawing board. Proving that finding one's passion begins with self-awareness, the next week a former subordinate called to ask if Mike would mentor him through some sales problems. As I said, it takes time for the subconscious to let go of what's familiar (Mike's idea that big and impersonal is best) and to accept what is unfamiliar (Mike's certainty that small and personal is best).

As mentioned earlier, Mike is part of the trend toward entrepreneurship that will continue to be the theme of the twenty-first century: people serving one another. There will also be plenty of job opportunities for older workers. The chart below indicates twenty categories of jobs for which the demand will grow over the next decades, according to a July 2008 Urban Institute policy paper written by researchers Gordon B. T. Mermin, Richard W. Johnson, and Eric J. Toder.[5]

Twenty Fastest-Growing Occupations for Older Workers

Occupation	Employment, 2007	Projected Change, 2006–2016 (%)	Share of Occupation's Workforce Ages 55+ (%)
Network systems and data communications analysts	382,356	53.4	5.7
Personal and home care aides	794,846	50.7	23.4
Personal financial advisors	343,170	40.9	18.8
Computer software engineers	869,358	37.8	9.1
Medical assistants	153,079	35.5	11.9
Veterinarians	66,824	35.5	22.4
Financial analysts	83,177	33.5	15.8
Commercial divers	10,256	33.3	0.0
Dental hygienists	154,575	29.9	11.0
Database administrators	94,436	29.4	8.7
Dental assistants	295,078	29.3	5.8
Computer systems analysts	277,001	29.0	13.9
Nursing, psychiatric, and home health aides	2,054,082	28.2	15.4
Physical therapist assistants and aides	74,098	28.0	4.3
Sales representatives, services, all other	598,020	27.8	12.4
Miscellaneous community and social service specialists	329,074	27.7	14.0
Network and computer systems administrators	178,344	27.2	7.3
Physical therapists	263,178	27.2	9.3
Miscellaneous personal appearance workers	230,296	26.4	7.3
Health diagnosing and treating practitioner support technicians	435,786	26.0	6.4
All 522 Occupations	153,751,169	10.0	16.6

SOURCE: Authors' computations from Bureau of Labor Statistics (2006) and Current Population Survey.
NOTE: Share of workers ages 55+ is the average for 2003–2007.

To show how lists like the preceding one can lead you to your passion, think of the auxiliary businesses that are spawned in each of these categories. Take veterinarians as an example. Now think of pets and all the jobs in the rapidly growing companion animal industry: jobs created by makers of pet food and accessories like collars and beds, drug manufacturers, and pet supply stores, and then there are breeders and judges of the dogs and cats who compete in show ring events, not to mention those who provide other services to pet owners.

One of my clients is a good example of how a personal interest in a growth occupation can turn into a business. Carol and her husband lived with a variety of animals. They even had a few pet snakes and geese. Carol often walked her neighbors' dogs when they were away, but it never occurred to her that she could make money doing this, until we talked about it during one of our sessions. "Why don't you get a dog-walking business card made?" I asked. "Then hand that out to your neighbors so they know you're doing this for a living now. I assure you, people who work all day and go on vacation will call you once they know you're available, since you're so trustworthy. Soon you'll have more business than you can handle."

And that is exactly what happened. Carol was astonished by the demand for her dog-walking service, which soon expanded to include pet sitting and pet feeding and watering services. Because she had so much business, she was able to quit her corporate job and soon had to hire several people. To prevent turnover, Carol paid her staff a premium hourly rate. Within a few years her business grossed six figures. Then she sold it to start a pet accessory business, which made her a true serial entrepreneur.

Your niche may be on the "Twenty Fastest-Growing Occupations" list, or it could be an adjunct to a category on it. If your niche is not on the list, don't let that discourage you. The categories from your phone book and the Internet are enough to get you started on your approach letters and emails.

The Approach Letter or Email

Now you're ready to meet with people in your categories of interest. Some of these people will say, "I did just what you're doing, and it worked!" Or you'll hear, "I wish I were doing what you're doing; is it really possible to find passion at my age and make money?" Once you're in the right niche, you'll hear, "You must be a genius; how did you figure this out?"

Getting out and talking with people is a good reality check. Sometimes all it takes is one visit before you decide to drop an interest from your list; in other cases you may need several meetings before you know the work is not for you. But each time, you get closer to what is right for you.

Even when you know the person you plan to call, send an approach letter or email to prepare her for your phone call. Cold calls to busy people are intrusive, like verbal spam. Think of how you'd like to be approached; ask yourself, "What would make me want to respond to this person?" Include your email address in your letters in case your contacts want to get back to you before you make the follow-up call.

The first paragraph in the letter or email describes in a couple of lines what you know about the person and the company, and it mentions who referred you (if you have a referral). The second paragraph talks about you and your experience, and why you're contacting this person. The third paragraph concludes with, "I realize you are busy, so I will call you in a few days to arrange a time to speak with you."

Paul, the finance expert I discussed in chapter 6, said his letters and emails made the sale before he called, meaning they were so well written that the recipients were open to scheduling a meeting with him. Some people asked Paul for help with their finances and investments, an unexpected response that led Paul to his passion: financial planning (note that this category is number three on the "Twenty Fastest-Growing Occupations" list).

Avoid typical job hunt procedures, such as responding to want ads or talking with recruiters — unless you want to work as a recruiter, as did Ann (discussed in the first chapter). Recruiters are helpful when you know what you want to do and when you need to know more about your target market. For now, you're just exploring options; so don't rush the process.

Study websites and other marketing material before you meet with your contacts. Read the bios and about the customer or client base. Notice your reaction to the website, layout, and design. Is the website focused, easy to read and navigate? Or is it poorly written and designed, with too much going on? (Look out, that's off-track signal #5, the most common cause of failure.)

If the person you plan to meet is local, drive by her place of business before your meeting. Walk in and look around, unless security prevents entry. That way, when you arrive at your destination the surroundings will feel familiar, making it easier for you to concentrate during your meeting.

Follow-Up Phone Calls

Mike knew that decision makers don't have much time to talk, so he got right to the point once he reached them. First, he thanked the person for taking his call, and then he asked if he or she had received his letter or email. If not, he offered to call back. If the person wanted to talk then and there, Mike recapped what he wrote and asked his first question (a list of interview questions appears later in this chapter).

Given today's automated phone systems, you'll probably need to leave a message when you call. Say why you're calling, and then repeat your name and number slowly (people get annoyed when they have to replay garbled or unclear phone messages). Let contacts know the best time to reach you, and then say you will call back in a few days if you don't hear from them.

If your call is not returned after a few more attempts, move on to the next person. The timing may be wrong, the person may be on vacation or out of the office, or he is not interested in speaking with you. Don't take this personally. Something may be going on with him — maybe he's thinking about leaving and doesn't want anyone to know. More likely, no response means he is not a match for you and what you want to do.

Most people feel a bit uneasy about setting up these meetings. "Why would they want to meet with me?" they ask me. The answer is that most people are glad to help if you're respectful of their time. They are curious too; they may want to do what you are doing! So don't be surprised by success.

For example, Kim said she was not expecting to be so comfortable when she met with people. "I feel so different in these meetings," Kim said when she called to give me an update on her progress. "Focusing on others really works."

"How would you have felt before?" I asked.

Kim thought for a moment and then said, "I would have been thinking about me, how I sounded, what kind of impression I was making. But after all the work I've done on myself, I'm fine with who I am. I ask a few questions, and the next thing I know they're telling me everything."

"In other words, they're comfortable because you're comfortable with yourself," I said.

"Yes. I used to think I had to explain myself, why I do things the way I do. It feels very odd to feel so secure."

"That's how you feel when you like yourself," I said.

"What a concept." Kim and I laughed, since not liking herself used to be her problem. (The happy ending to Kim's story comes later in this chapter.)

After you meet with a few people, go back over your strengths, values, and needs to see if anything has changed. When job opportunities failed to excite Mike, he realized he didn't want to work for a company after all. So he repositioned himself as a sales troubleshooter for individual clients.

Then a former sales colleague called to say that he was the vice president of sales at a new company. He asked if Mike would be interested in helping him with sales. The next week Mike's most recent employer, the owner with unrealistic expectations, called to ask if Mike would come back! Now Mike had several options: he could help his colleague build sales; structure an independent relationship with his old boss, his first client, so to speak; or work with his own clients. Whatever he chose, he could use the experience as material for his book.

But as time went by, Mike noticed he didn't really want to follow up on the opportunities offered by his previous employers or colleagues (remember, lack of enthusiasm means it's not your passion), so he paused to rethink his list of values, strengths, and goals, revising them to match what he really wanted to do. Then out of the blue (right), Brad, another former boss, called Mike to talk about a new trend in the marketing business, promoting businesses that are concerned about the environment. "Making good use of resources is the new industrial revolution," Mike told me excitedly when he called to talk about the latest turn in his journey. "It's called sustainability." When I asked for an example of sustainability, Mike told me about a carpet company that had trouble competing with other firms, since everyone appeared to offer the same service. With the help of sustainability marketing experts, the carpet company owners changed their business model.

"They advertised that they not only sold and installed carpet but also recycled the old carpeting," Mike said. "And for a monthly fee they maintained the existing carpet. As carpet squares deteriorated, they replaced them at no further cost. In addition, 100 percent of the company's old carpet is recycled back into new carpet, even if it was installed by another company. So there is zero waste, which appeals to customers." Mike added that sooner or later all businesses will need to promote a clean environments, or customers will go elsewhere. "Brad and I plan to combine my sales experience with his marketing expertise to help businesses get ahead of that curve before their competitors."

A month later Mike called to say a sustainability expert had approached his team, which had now expanded to include two more consultants. "He's really impressed with the business model we've put together. But I told Brad he wouldn't work out, because he wants to be the star. He doesn't understand that in business the customer is the star. I was surprised Brad didn't see what was obvious to me, but then he's a consultant not a sales guy."

The work Mike had done on himself taught him to appreciate what he used to take for granted. "You know how it is, you assume people know what you know," Mike said, laughing. "But they don't. We just invoiced our first paying client, but we need to generate more revenues, so I'm writing content for our new website. This project has helped me to know what I want to say in my book on sales, so I'm starting on that project. Another former employee contacted me recently about helping him get a job, and since coaching is an option that really interests me, I agreed to work with him for several sessions. Funny thing is, I fired this man before because he was close-minded. I guess when you're paying for good advice you listen."

If you look at Mike's collage in chapter 6, you'll see that it illustrated his perfect niche: a simple, self-directed life. This is an example of how the passion process works. You start with one goal, in Mike's case finding a better boss. Then the process shifts as you shift. For Mike, this meant working alone as a sales coach for individuals, writing about that process, and helping his partners develop sustainable marketing strategies for companies.

To make choices that match your collage, ask the people you interview what they do during a typical day. How much time do they spend alone and with others? What problems do they solve? How are they paid? Ask if their business model targets a particular segment of the market, or do they go after many markets? (Don't work with companies that try to be all things to all people.)

As an outsider you can see what insiders may be too close to see.

This is why companies recruit experienced CEOs, even in the early stages of development, since founders are not always the best managers. Think about a time when you asked an outsider to look at some aspect of your life. For example, you may have asked a real estate agent to assess your property's marketability. After a walk-through, perhaps the agent suggested that you hire a stager to improve your home's appearance. Did you see the merit in the agent's suggestion and in the stager's expertise? If so, were you pleased with the results? Did you take the stager's ideas with you into your new home?

Think of yourself as a stager when you meet people. Look to see how you could improve what they're doing. Sometimes this is a small change, but what you suggest they do makes the difference between success and failure.

Sometimes people will go off on tangents in your meetings. When this happens, bring their attention back to what you need to know. After thirty minutes, thank them for their time, then ask them whether it would be all right to meet again if you find you have more questions. Don't be surprised when people want to prolong your meetings. It's okay to stay a while longer, but don't wear out your welcome. Better that people want more time with you than no more time at all. You can always come back for a second or third meeting if there's mutual interest.

Before you meet with experts, offer to pay for their time. If these people are the positive experts described in chapter 4, off-track signal #4, don't hesitate to open your checkbook. They will save you time, money, and grief.

Speak and Write Clearly

Before you hit the send button or put your approach letters in envelopes, read them out loud. Does the writing sound like you, or is the language too casual or too formal? If so, rewrite until the letter sounds like you. Letters and emails can be easy to misconstrue, because the reader doesn't have the benefit of face-to-face contact.

Stick to plain English: subject, verb, then object, and go easy on the adjectives and adverbs. Check for spelling and punctuation errors. Sloppiness indicates you don't care enough to get it right, and this spells trouble for any company. In this age of hastily written emails, a well-crafted personal note on the best stationery makes a good impression.

Print out the letters and the outside of envelopes unless your handwriting is outstanding, and use a commemorative stamp. If you send an email, write the email in three short paragraphs with spaces between the paragraphs. Here is an example of an approach email a client sent to a man she knew through her work as an engineer. Eric is a professor as well as a writer and consultant.

Hello Eric,

I want to first of all congratulate you on the publication of your new book. You must feel very proud and happy to see your work in print. I am sure readers will appreciate your insight and knowledge.

I am writing to you because you are not only an industry insider, but you also teach a subject that immensely interests me. And since you have just published a book on the subject of product development, meeting with you would be very helpful to me.

My purpose at this point is to gather information so I can make a better decision about my career and to be sure I am not overlooking things. I know my strengths and values and am fairly sure of what I would like to do, but would appreciate your perspective.

I will call you in a day or two to set up a time to get together that is convenient for you.

Sincerely,
Lesley

Eric wrote back before Lesley could follow up, saying that it was great to hear from her. He thanked her for her kind words and gave her two dates that were convenient for him.

When you meet with people, listen to how they answer your questions. Are they direct or evasive? When do you or they feel excited (passion clue)? If you miss something, ask the person to repeat the point.

Before you leave, ask for names of people they respect who would be helpful to you. Ask if you can use their names when you contact these references. Let them know you'll approach others with emails or letters and then phone calls.

When it's appropriate, offer to take people to breakfast or lunch. During the meal, be conscious of time and don't ask too much from them. Breakfast is better when people are too busy for lunch, and it's less expensive. Get up at dawn if that's what it takes to meet a passionate person. If you can solve their problems, they might pay for your breakfast!

Your First Meeting

You sent your letter or email; you followed up with a phone call; the person agreed to meet with you. You are excited and nervous. Good. These are positive signs.

If you expect that everyone you meet will have it all together, you'll find you dispose of that assumption after a few meetings. With some people, you may even find yourself in the role of career counselor. Many of my clients are startled by how much they know because of the work they have done on themselves. This was true for Kim, who was surprised by her self-assurance. But even though you may be ahead in terms of self-awareness, you will learn from everyone you meet, even if it's only how unconscious some people are. Some will tell you more than you want to know; others' frustrations will make you laugh. One cruise company owner told one of my clients, "This would be a great business if it weren't for the passengers."

A few people will feel threatened by you. After one client told an "expert" what she wanted to do, he responded by saying, "Oh, that's an idea I've heard several times this year. Must be an idea whose time has come and gone." Others you meet will be afraid of the unknown. "I'd do what you're doing too, but the economy is not that great right now."

When a meeting is not going well, don't argue or try to explain. Just say, "Thank you for your time," and leave. Regardless of what happens, send a thank-you note or email the next day.

Dress appropriately, in clothing neither too casual nor too dressy. First impressions do make an impact, so leave the jangling jewelry, strong perfume or aftershave, excessive makeup, and loud colors at home. You want people to remember you as someone they enjoyed meeting, not someone they would prefer not to see again.

Wear colors that bring out the best in you. If your complexion is fair, don't wear orange, for example, or pastels when you're the dark, dramatic type. Black, gray, and blue are good basic colors, and they bespeak authority. If you're in the fashion or art world, your appearance should reflect a sense of style.

On the whole, you'll enjoy your meetings, and people will enjoy meeting you. After a few meetings you'll realize you have done this all your life; you just didn't call it interviewing. Whatever happens, flow with events, as Kim did. Kim went to one of her meetings with recruitment businesses only to learn that the office manager, her contact, had been called out of the office. As she talked with the receptionist, they hit it off so well that Kim decided to ask this woman, Cindy, to lunch.

During lunch, Kim asked Cindy about the young owner of the company. "She's the smartest woman I know," Cindy said admiringly. "Her mind works so fast it's scary. She's known as the best in what she does."

Then Kim asked how the owner handled the demands on her time. "I think she gets overwhelmed sometimes," Cindy said. "She says she wishes she had more time to research candidates' backgrounds as thoroughly as she would like to do."

Since resourcefulness was one of Kim's top strengths, she felt excited about meeting the office manager. This is an example of the problems you get to hear about in low-pressure meetings. People tell you what's going on because you're not asking them to hire you.

Kim began her meeting with Barbara, the office manager, by saying how impressed she was with Cindy. Barbara agreed, saying that many people had tried to recruit Cindy. Next, Kim asked about the business. After Barbara answered the questions, she asked Kim why she was interested in recruiting.

Kim said that, at her stage of life (midfifties), she wanted to use her research skills in work that matched her values, particularly her love of intellectual stimulation, variety, and independence.

"Do you think these values can be met in recruiting?" Kim asked Barbara.

"Definitely. In fact, you and the owner have the same values," Barbara said, and then she looked toward the back of the office. "Wait here a minute and I'll ask if she's available. I want her to meet you."

After she shook hands with the owner, Kim said she didn't want to interrupt her day, but she would like to learn more about her business. Could they meet again at the owner's convenience? "Yes, of course," the young owner said, looking at her schedule. "How about next Tuesday afternoon at three?"

Kim sent follow-up emails to Cindy, Barbara, and the owner the next day, complimenting them on their courtesy and enthusiasm and summarizing what she had learned in the meetings. She ended by saying she looked forward to learning more about the business.

At the end of their next meeting, the owner asked Kim if she would like to do research assignments on a part-time basis. "Barbara will train you in the basics," the owner said.

"I would like that very much," Kim said excitedly. The next week Kim started her new job. Today, she's a valued member of the company's team.

On average, it takes about fifteen meetings before the Aha! moment occurs, when you know this is it. This can happen when you least expect it. So do what Kim did: trust your intuition. Her impromptu lunch with Cindy revealed the problem Kim could solve using strengths she had developed over a lifetime. The meeting with Barbara confirmed that the recruiting business was the right niche. The meeting with the owner ended with an offer.

An added plus was that Kim could work from her home office as a virtual assistant on a contract basis, two of the must-haves on her needs list. Essentially, she was one solo serving another solo type, but within the framework of a team. Kim might have been rejected had she sent a résumé, since her background was not in the recruiting business.

In chapter 2 I said that today's employers, especially owners of small businesses, are open to hiring older, smart, productive people. Face-to-face meetings that you arrange through referrals are always preferable to typical job search strategies, particularly when you want to work in an entrepreneurial as opposed to a corporate environment.

Caroline's Story

Setting up low-pressure meetings also worked for Caroline. She met with several people to see if selling, buying, or remodeling properties was what she wanted to do. One meeting was with a broker whose office was near Caroline's home. After she discussed her values and strengths, and before she could say anything else, the broker started talking about his need for people who could connect with high-end customers. "They would want to work with you," he told her.

Caroline had been a model in her younger years, and she still had the poise that had made her at ease on the runway. She also had a sense of humor and an engaging personality, so it's no wonder the broker was eager to bring her on board. "After you meet with a few of my top salespeople," he said, "let's talk again."

When Caroline called to talk with me about the meeting, she was so excited we both thought this was the right niche for her, although I wondered how Caroline would cope with her customers' slow decision-making processes. After several more meetings, she decided to keep her current sales job while she studied for the real estate exam. Once she passed it and got her license, she quit her job and went to work with the broker's company. The real estate company offered training and support, but Caroline said she would not have survived the first year had she not done the inner work. "Every day I see the payoff for all that self-scrutiny," Caroline said to me. "I'm so glad I took the time to look at my past before I went forward. The Drama Triangle is everywhere I go. My clients have so many problems. I'm sympathetic but I stay detached."

Caroline's perseverance paid off with sales and personal growth in her first year. "Whatever happens, this work has forced me to set boundaries," Caroline said midway through her second year. "My husband and son have noticed the change in me. I was a marshmallow before, and I know that's why I was always angry. Anger was how I protected myself, but all that did was make me feel like a Victim."

A year later, after a slowdown in sales, Caroline was rethinking her decision to get into real estate. "In our last conversation you said I was frustrated because I'm not selling a product, that real estate sales is a service," Caroline said. "You also said I need to enjoy the process. The truth is, I hate this process. And some of my customers resent having to pay a commission, as though I don't earn it. And another thing," Caroline added, getting worked up, "there is no loyalty in this business. I asked an agent in my office to finish up a sale for me while I was on vacation. She said she would be glad to help, but when I got back she had stolen my client!"

"Well, I'd say hating the process and being taken advantage of by greedy colleagues are both off-track signals," I said. "What did you like about selling products?"

"I loved calling on my customers," Caroline said. "I didn't have to wait for people to call me. I sold to vineyard operations managers who either needed the equipment or they didn't need it, at least not then. I see now that I need to represent something tangible."

"That would probably be for someone you already know, Caroline," I said.

"It's funny you should say that. A vineyard worker approached me about a tool he's invented," Caroline said. "He wants me to figure out how to bring it to market. I was so jazzed after we talked that I got online to research patent and prototype information."

"Feeling jazzed and working for free are passion clues," I said, and we laughed.

"Maybe his tool is the first product in a sales rep business," I added.

Caroline was excited after she attended a class on how to market inventions. She said the instructor had put her in touch with a former student who had created a product for the wine industry. Within weeks Caroline was representing the product. But that was simply a step that led to other potential clients. When Caroline came by a few months later to update me on her progress, I asked, "Now that you can be more objective, why do you think you got into real estate sales?"

"Money," Caroline said without hesitation. "I thought I could make the big bucks, and then I could do what I wanted to do." When she saw the surprised look on my face, Caroline threw up her hands. "I know, I know, that's opposite of the way you say to do it. But getting into real estate got rid of my belief that there is a quick and easy way to get rich. You can be sure I'm taking that learning with me into my new enterprise."

Ah, yes, this is a changed woman!

Caroline called a few weeks later while driving between appointments with new customers. "It's raining cats and dogs out here, and I'm having the time of my life! I just thought you'd want to know that I'm loving the process," she said, laughing. Caroline had to come full circle to discover that she would succeed only when she put enjoyment of the process ahead of making money (passion clue).

Interview Questions

Take the following list of questions with you when you meet with people. After you leave, make note of the questions that stirred up the most interest, both in you and the other person.

POSITIVE PERSONAL QUESTIONS

- What do you like best about your work?
- How has doing the work changed you as a person?
- What has your work taught you about people and yourself?

POSITIVE COMPANY QUESTIONS

- What do you like about the owner or president of your company?
- How does this person inspire trust?
- Why is your company (or practice) successful?

POSITIVE INDUSTRY QUESTIONS

- Who is the best in the industry and why?
- What positive trends do you see?
- What makes your industry recession-proof?

Next are lists of questions that reveal problems.

PROBLEMATIC PERSONAL QUESTIONS

- What do you dislike about your work?
- What would you change if you could?
- What prevents you from doing this?

PROBLEMATIC COMPANY QUESTIONS

- What costs are incurred by government regulation?
- How do you attract and keep good people?
- How does the company deal with incompetent workers?

PROBLEMATIC INDUSTRY QUESTIONS

- How do government regulations affect your industry?
- How has your industry changed from five years ago?
- How is your industry affected by downturns in the economy?

The answers to these questions reveal the problems you can solve if you're interested. When, for example, Kim heard that the owner of the recruiting firm was overwhelmed by demands on her time, she knew her resourcefulness could solve that problem.

Email or mail a thank-you note the day after your meeting that says what you learned and that you will let the person know the outcome of your search. Everyone likes to know if something they did or said helped you to succeed.

Wrapping Up

Some of my clients get right to the close and then back off, waiting to be asked. Women especially are reluctant to ask for what they want, because they're afraid of being seen as pushy, or they fear rejection, or they don't know their value. Men can be passive in closing circumstances if they're ambivalent about what they want, or if their egos get in the way ("They [the potential employers] should ask *me*"). A typical closing conversation begins with your contact person saying to you, "Now that you've met everyone, what do you think about working with me (or the company)?"

After the owner of the recruiting company asked Kim to do part-time research, she said, "When do I start?" Caroline did not hesitate to say yes when she was asked to represent products. But strangely enough, once she detached from her desire to make money, Caroline's real estate sales started picking up and her relationships with clients and other agents improved. She had also developed a mutually respectful relationship with an investor who bought foreclosed properties. He liked and trusted Caroline, so he asked her to find buyers for these houses. Her willingness to adjust to these positive signals from the marketplace was an indication of Caroline's emotional and spiritual growth. Not that her motives were truly selfless; but she put solving others' problems ahead of her personal gain, and the outside world adjusted to mirror that inner change.

Résumés

A good résumé is concise, error-free, and no more than two pages. And if you know what you want to do and the people you want to do it for, you can tailor your résumé to the specific opportunity, eliminating the catchall subhead *Objective* that begins many résumés. Use only two fonts, plus bold and italics for section heads and outstanding achievements.

Phrases like "self-motivated problem-solver" and "excellent verbal and written communication skills" are obsolete. You need to give the readers of your résumé specific examples of *how* you solved a problem, and *why* your communication skills led to success, such as: "Because of my ability to establish trust with customers, they told me they were not getting what they needed from my company. So I created a feedback survey that became a company-wide practice, increasing revenue and customer satisfaction."

Arrange awards and achievements by bullet points, and, again, be specific with numbers and percentages that demonstrate the problems you solve easily and well, specifically the strategies you used to build strong teams and increase sales, efficiency, revenues, and brand recognition. Don't include volunteer efforts from earlier years; instead focus on the last several years. It is common these days to include links to personal websites or social networking links, and this helps employers to know more about you. But be selective about the kind of information you put online, since you never know who is going to read it.

Never, ever lie on your résumé. Telling the truth will get you into the niche with the right amount of challenge, whereas lies (including omissions) will get you into a place that is over your head, and then you'll disappoint people. Explain any gaps in your history, such as when you were handling family business, working for yourself, looking for a job, or taking a sabbatical.

If you were fired from a position, be honest about why you were fired. Many top-notch people have been fired and have then gone on to great achievements, so don't be embarrassed about failure. Failure forces all of us to become wiser, more thoughtful people. When we only know success, we get lazy and complacent. What matters is your attitude about failure. If you learn from it and turn failure to your advantage, others will admire your character.

Include a personalized cover letter with your résumé that shows why you are a match for the opening. This is your chance to elaborate on any qualifications and experience not covered in the résumé. Two or three short paragraphs will do, well spaced, written on quality stationery and in the same font as the résumé.

If you're asked for art, design, or writing samples, select your best work. Writing samples should be in the same style as the rest of your material: your cover letter and bio or résumé. Disjointed, mismatched presentations reveal that this is how you think. Impeccable presentations say you exceed expectations even before you're hired, that you are an "A" player.

If asked, include reference letters. Call your references to let them know what the job requires, so they'll be prepared for the hiring person's call. References are typically checked at the end of the interviewing stage, so don't give references until you've decided the job or project is what you want to do. In other words, you'll want to do your reference checks on them!

For examples of résumés and how to respond online, I recommend Joyce Lain Kennedy's *Resumes for Dummies*.[6]

Proposals

Proposals are used when you want to create a job or a contract position, as when you provide your services for a fee. You also need to write a proposal when you submit a business plan, a prototype to a manufacturer or distributor, a book idea to an agent or editor, or an application for a grant.

Check with Google for links to proposal-writing sites if you need help with content, format, and style. But do your own draft first so that you're not overly influenced by what you read.

If you want to write a grant proposal, study examples on foundation websites. Or take a class on grant writing at the local community college or university extension program. You can also talk with people who read proposals for a living. You can find these people in your phone book or online. When in doubt, trust your intuition to select the person who "feels right."

Before you write a proposal, be sure you know the motivations of your intended audience. Don't let your ego or personal and political prejudices cloud your judgment. The best proposal causes a reader to say, "I like this. It works. Let's do it!"

One of my clients wanted to write a grant proposal to create a Marriage Savers group in her area. Margaret's own marriage was successful, and the relationship was a source of stability in her life and the lives of her children, unlike what she had experienced in childhood. Helping others to achieve and maintain a mutually respectful marriage was Margaret's passion. Putting on seminars for married or about-to-be-married couples would be a good use of her natural teaching and counseling skills. Running the program would use her organizational strengths. She was also a good writer, a reflection of her practical mind.

Since her state had a high divorce rate, Margaret wrote to the governor, local officials, pastors, and marriage counselors to gain support. To her delight, they loved her idea. Inspired by their enthusiasm, she wrote a proposal in which she set goals she could reach. Later, the program expanded as word spread about its value to participants. "My life today looks just like my collage. I never dreamed I would be in charge of a program that means so much to me," Margaret wrote to me a couple of years after her program had become a fixture in her community.

Margaret was an executive assistant when she first called me, a job she had taken to supplement family income, she said. After I read her story, it was obvious what she should do. The pattern was there, as it is in every story. But she lacked confidence, so I suggested she stay with the job she had while she researched and worked on the proposal. Her husband agreed with this approach. I've found that it's vital that their partners support my clients in their efforts; otherwise the relationship will suffer. Fortunately, most people want their partners to love their work.

"In our first conversation, you said I wouldn't succeed until I got to the head of the line," Margaret said. "I was so scared when I heard you say that, but you were right. Being in charge feels great!"

Like many people, Margaret was not aware that others would pay for what she did for free. Couples were always coming to her house to talk about their marriages; many told her she should be a marriage counselor. But Margaret preferred the managerial role, since she was a team type. The problem was that Margaret thought she was not qualified to lead, a decision she'd made while growing up with a stepfather who often told her she was stupid (now that was a projection!). Yet throughout her life, Margaret always took the initiative. Even as a child she was adventuresome.

"You're the one with the passion and the common sense, so you should lead the way," I said.

Then Margaret said a few local marriage counselors and pastors had volunteered to add their names to her proposal if she would take charge. They all thought she was a good writer and that she should put the idea forward. "Then your only obstacle is you," I said, and we laughed.

If you're a writer and you want to publish an article, read several is-sues of your target publication. If you're a beginner, start with lesser-known publications, because that way you'll have less competition. You can find these publications in the latest edition of *The Writer's Market* in the reference section in your local library. I also recommend *Jeff Herman's Guide to Book Publishers, Editors, and Literary Agents* for an agent's take on the publishing business.

To create an Internet blog as a business, go to Problogger.net for instructions. The pull-down menu on the home page is full of tips on style, content, and how to get advertisers. As experts say, the stronger your voice, the more chance you have of making money as a blogger, especially when your target audience and advertisers have your values.

Before you write a proposal to agents or publishers, study their websites to make sure they represent your topic. Agents and publishers' websites often give examples of how to write and submit proposals, and they offer tips on getting accepted. When you're rejected, this could mean your work is not right for the person you submitted it to or that you need to do more work on it. After a few different agents or pub-lishers reject your work, ask someone you know to read your manu-script or, better yet, hire an editor.

A professional eye can see what you're doing that is not working. The problem may be as simple as having the wrong title, meaning the concept of the book is not yet clear to you, as was the case with my first book (and this book as well).

What follows is the query letter I wrote to the person who would become my publisher (Marc Allen at New World Library) after I came up with the right title. This letter was written in 1983 in the middle of a seemingly endless recession, long before the idea of passion in your work and doing what you love became popular. Although part of me was shaking in my shoes, it was exciting to be a scout for the future.

Dear Marc,

The first law of money is: do what you love; the money will follow. Most Americans are not in the right work and don't have the tools to discover their passion and how to make money at it. For over seven years I have worked as a career consultant in my own business in San Francisco helping individuals find the work they love. Before this business I was a journalist, interviewing and writing about subjects from hard news to features. I have combined my two passions, counseling and writing, to inspire others to achieve what I have. The result is my book, titled *Work with Passion: How to Do What You Love for a Living*.

This book fills an ever-present need — to find productive work that makes you happy. The audience for this book will be all who earn their living and who want the satisfaction of a career they like so much that they'd do it for nothing, but do not. They get paid, and well. I have enclosed an outline, preface, and first chapter for your perusal. The book is finished.

I have selected you because of the work you have done with Gawain's *Creative Visualization* and Ross's *Prospering Woman*. The layout, editing, and design are exactly what I want. I think my book is the next logical step for you, from visualizing, to prosperity consciousness, to working with passion. Thank you for considering my book.

Regards,
Nancy Anderson

P.S. I have enclosed a tape of a recent KGO Radio guest spot to give you an idea of how I come across. Promotion of the book is very important to me. I want very much to be involved in marketing the product I believe in so strongly.

I jumped for joy the day the office manager called to ask me to send the rest of the manuscript. Twenty-plus years later, the book is still selling.

Offers

Offers should be slow in coming, unless you're the answer to a company's prayer. Even then, be wary of quick closes. Hasty hiring decisions can be costly for everyone. If people take more time than you expect, see the delay as good for you and them. Stay in touch, but don't besiege people; they will think you're desperate.

Even when you're sure that you'll get an offer, continue with your meetings. Circumstances change. One of my clients thought she had an offer, and then someone with much more experience applied for the job at the last minute. Emily was angry when she heard the company had hired the other person. A month later she heard the person had backed out the day before starting because he wanted to stay with his current employer. By then Emily had decided the job required too much travel. This is an example of how delays work to your advantage.

Look at websites like Salary.com to see what's typical for your geographic area and experience. To find the going rate for your services by the hour or project, check with others in your field to see what they charge. In a free market, remember, what you're paid depends on the *buyer's* perception of your value. The tendency is to undervalue work when it is easy for you, as when your insight penetrates to the core of a problem.

In any case start with the figure that feels right to you. If it's too high, you'll feel pressured to produce results beyond your capabilities. If the price is too low, you'll feel resentful about giving away your time. You can always raise your price when you have more business than you can handle.

Dana, for example, did not know her value until she started a coaching business that included health and weight loss management for women. She was a nurse as well as an esthetician and a certified life coach, an unusual combination that she used to help women live healthy, balanced lives and have fun reaching that goal. Previously, Dana had owned a landscaping business, and then a skin-care and massage salon, but as she aged, working outdoors became too strenuous for her, and one-on-one work in the salon was too confining. I suggested that she consider coaching, since that work would use her mind and she could do it for a long time (an example of right livelihood).

Dana thought she was an extroverted, team-type personality when we met. But chronic physical ailments indicated she was spending far too much time with people; she was playing the Rescuer role at home and work. Coaching others via telephone from her home office set a clear boundary between Dana and her clients, the perfect niche for a smart introvert.

"It's so true that you teach what you need to learn," Dana said, laughing, when she talked to me about her new practice. "All of my clients take on more than they can handle, and then they wonder why they're so exhausted. Like you say, overdoing it is a national disease. What's amazing is that my life today is just like the images in my collage: balanced and peaceful."

When interviewing for a job, if you're asked about salary requirements, be truthful. Don't waste employers' time if the income is less than what you want and deserve. The exception is when the opportunity will increase your knowledge or confidence.

Before you accept an offer, say you'd like to think about it overnight or over the weekend. Talk with your spouse or partner; review your strengths, values, and needs to see if the offer matches your template for success. If it does, accept.

Before you leave your old job, write a short resignation letter to your employer or boss, saying how much you appreciated the opportunity to work there. If your employer or boss makes a counteroffer, turn it down no matter what you're offered. If you stay, your loyalty will be forever suspect. After all, you would not be leaving if the job and associations were right for you.

Always go out on top when you leave any situation, being thankful for what you learned.

SUMMARY

1. Know your relationship type: partner, team, or solo.
2. Do your homework.
3. Focus on the process, not the outcome.
4. Look for the problems you solve easily and well.
5. Take the opportunity that makes you grow.

CHAPTER 8

Savor Success on Your Terms

I have no home: I make awareness my home.
— ANONYMOUS SAMURAI, FOURTEENTH CENTURY

Now it is time to celebrate the happy ending, otherwise known as unfamiliar territory. You are in your perfect niche, working as a partner, team, or solo type, as an introvert or an extrovert. You are amazed that others pay you to do what you love so much that you would do the work for nothing.

Letting go of the self-destructive script that kept you mired in the past was not easy. I bet there were times when the middle stage of change dragged on and on (and on) so long you thought it would never end. But just look at you now: how different you are from the person who began the journey to passion. Those who "knew you when" may not recognize the person you see when you look in the mirror.

As with any change, you will need to allow time to adjust to new circumstances. Even if you succeeded in the past, your perfect niche will seem strange and unfamiliar. If you were always disappointed in the past, trying but never reaching your heart's desire, you will need even more time to get used to success. After all, failure is what your subconscious thought was "just the way life is." Struggling is so familiar that it's hard to imagine not struggling anymore. What do you do now that you are out of the cocoon?

The Downside of Success

I would be remiss if I didn't warn you about the downside of success, particularly envy, jealousy, and rivalry. These darkest of human emotions wreak havoc in relationships at home and work. If you ignore or don't want to see the truth about human nature, envy or rivalry will blindside you when you least expect it, especially when it comes from people who are close to you. As you know, some human beings tend to have an ambivalent attitude about people who are happy *and* financially secure. When you're miserable and broke, nearly everybody sympathizes with you. But once you achieve material and spiritual success, some people will feel uncomfortable around you. Others can hardly wait for you to fall (a few may give you a push!).

Success is a magnet that attracts people who admire you and want to be just like you. Success also attracts people who want to pull you down. Others will play on your sympathy with sad stories, hoping that you'll make the process of reaching their goals easier for them than it was for you. Look out. Feeling guilty about your success is a script that will hook you into the Rescuer role in the Drama Triangle, a compassion trap with no exit. The next thing you know, you'll feel angry about being used, and then you'll be in the Persecutor role, blaming others for your lack of boundaries. This also puts you in the role of the Victim of the person who victimized you, which will take you down, down, down into the pit of despair.

Being on the receiving end of envy is not as painful if you remember how you felt when others got what you wanted. Did their achievement stir up feelings of resentment? Was it hard to be around these people? Did you find yourself criticizing people who had what you wanted, taking perverse pleasure in mentally bringing them down to size? Were you secretly glad when they failed or made mistakes? If so, you know what it's like to be the target of envy.

Envy is an emotion that reduces in size after you admit that you feel it. Pretending that you're not envious when you are only increases envy, or pretense sends envy down into the subconscious, where it festers into resentment and bitterness. As I've said previously, feelings just want to be felt by you. Self-acceptance includes accepting *all* of your emotions, not just the positive emotions. Then you are a balanced, whole individual.

Envy can be used in a healthy way. For example, notice what causes you to feel envious. This will help you to identify what you would like to have in your life. It will also reveal what you need to do in order to achieve the results you desire.

It also helps to remember the successful people who encouraged you. Were they patient even when you lost heart? Did they offer help and guidance and, at the same time, let you struggle so that you could gain confidence? This is the person you will be now, the wise, loving individual who appreciates the value of the struggle.

You will also need time to prepare for the increased responsibility that accompanies success. Everybody expects more of you now. Your actions have to match your words so that you don't disappoint the people who look up to you. When you make a mistake, you'll need to correct it immediately so that molehills remain molehills.

Excessive pride is another challenge of success. This happens when you take success for granted. You forget the trials and setbacks you endured and those who helped you along the way. After enough people tell you how great you are, you start to believe them. Vanity is always lurking in the background of your psyche, waiting for you to give in to its ceaseless craving for adulation.

Mick LaSalle, the aforementioned movie critic for the *San Francisco Chronicle*, has written insightfully about the tragic downside to success:

> The whole trying-to-live-up-to-a-persona thing — trying to mold yourself into some publicly accepted idea of who you are — is the ultimate self-effacement. It's the ultimate trap, too. When you see

[an example of this], you can better understand the vehemence
with which many celebrities fight against being typed. People all
want to be loved, and people tend to emphasize the things about
themselves that they're loved for. It takes discipline and an ironclad
sense of self to pull back from love and simply locate oneself, especially in the face of widespread acclaim and adulation. When
artists can't do that, they cease to be functioning artists. That's
how fame wrecks people.[1]

Having an ironclad sense of self is vital not just for artists but also
for you when your achievements put you in the public eye, regardless
of how small the audience. You will need to navigate the peak of the
mountain carefully, not getting too close to the edge.

As the proverb says, "Pride goes before destruction, a haughty
spirit before a fall." So if you find yourself getting enamored with the
money and acclaim, those are signs you are tempting fate. Be modest
about your achievements, and kind to those who are on the way up, for
you will surely meet them on your way down.

The Upside to Success

Happily, there are many upsides to success, chief of which are self-
respect and lightheartedness. You know what you had to sacrifice to be
where you are, and you're proud of the person you've become. You go
to sleep at night knowing that you won't repeat certain choices, no matter who pressures you to make them. You hold yourself to a higher standard than most because you know that what goes around comes around
in exact measure. Now that your faith has been rewarded, you don't
take life so seriously. Nor do you have to convince yourself by con-
vincing others, so you take their skepticism in stride.

Before you start your new life, review what it took to get you where
you are, the victories as well as the defeats that you never have to experience again. Repetition has been called the mother of learning, but
thoroughness is the father of success.

Review the Journey

Do you remember how you felt when you read the opening paragraph in the first chapter of *Work with Passion in Midlife and Beyond*?

> Ann was like most of the seventy-eight million people who are in or beyond midlife: she wanted to use her talent and experience in work that would give her life meaning and purpose (passion clue!) and to make all the money she needed. Her goal was to wake up every morning looking forward to a new day of challenge and growth. But she wasn't sure how to make that dream a reality — she didn't know the specific steps to take and in what order to take them.

Had you known what you would have to go through and how long it would take, would you have started the journey to passion in midlife and beyond? Most likely your answer back then would have been "No way!" But now that you're here, you are glad you took the first step into the unknown.

Step One

The first step into the unknown was to admit that what you were doing wasn't working and to ask for help if you needed it. At that point you may have hired a coach or a counselor to keep you accountable.

Perhaps you teamed up with a passion buddy to share the journey, or you took classes from experts in the field that interested you. You may have joined a support group. When you felt tired, they reminded you that change is a process.

During the first stage of change, you identified which of the six basic fears kept you up at night: the fear of poverty, loss of love, criticism, illness, old age, or death. The more you faced these scary ghosts head on, the more you realized they were products of an overly active imagination.

Step Two

The next step into the unknown was eliminating everything that interfered with clear thinking: habits like drinking, working, or doing too much; clutter; and outdated possessions. You went through every room, closet, and drawer in your house or apartment, and your garage and storage unit, until all that was left was what you used and loved.

As you walked around your streamlined surroundings, you felt so relieved you wondered why you waited so long to start the slimming process. You may have moved to a smaller, less demanding space. With passion in midlife and beyond as your goal, less was definitely more.

Once clutter, obsolete possessions, and bad habits were out of the way, you took a hard look at the people in your life to see who was draining time, money, and energy, and who was giving as much as they were taking. Removing yourself from some of these relationships was more difficult than you expected.

However, as you drew better boundaries, some people left your life on their own; in other cases, you were the one who did the leaving. At first you wondered if you made the right decision, if you could have done something differently, or if you were too hasty. But time proved that you did what was right for all concerned.

Step Three

The third step into the unknown was to rewrite your life script, beginning with your grandparents' and parents' scripts and what they experienced regarding money, work, and relationships. To gain objectivity, you referred to everyone in the story by their first names.

As you wrote, parents came down off their pedestals and onto the earth with you. It may have been painful to let go of a child's idealized (and highly charged) view of the family. But what you gained was an adult's perspective. By the time you got to your birth, you knew how your story was going to end if you didn't change your script.

Writing about childhood and teen years helped you become aware of when and why you decided that your life was not going to end well. You made this decision, or series of decisions, when you were too young to know what you were doing, based on one of three illogical assumptions: "What's the use? I'll never be happy," or "I can't be happy if they're not happy," or "If it weren't for them I would be happy."

You learned that these generalizations put you in the roles of the Victim, Rescuer, and Persecutor in the Drama Triangle, a game whose goal is failure for all parties. You were shocked when you realized what you had done to yourself and what you had allowed others to do to you. But now you do your best to be honest and direct in your communication, instead of dishonest and indirect.

In spite of your best intentions, when you got angry or impatient you found yourself going back to what was familiar. "Oh, no, not again. I thought I was done with this," you exclaimed to yourself, particularly when your brain translated painful emotions into bodily pain.

Muscle spasms, migraine headaches, or other tension-related ailments were signs you needed to talk to your brain, to remind it once again that you wanted to feel anger and anxiety rather than displace these painful emotions into your body. You may relapse occasionally, but the correction time is becoming quicker and quicker.

Next you wrote about how you navigated the stages in your life from teen years into adulthood, through college, military, and/or work experiences. You included romances, marriages, divorces, children, jobs, businesses, and creative projects. As you studied your experiences, you noticed the pattern that ran through the story: The choices that turned out well were based on internal motivation. The choices that did not work were externally motivated: the need for approval, money, sex, or power.

The conflicts you had with authority figures turned out to be a repeat of your interaction with your father, or from not having a father who took a genuine interest in you and who succeeded in the work he loved. But the more self-disciplined you became, the less you needed a father figure to tell you what to do. Trusting yourself ended conflicts with authority figures, including your father, even if he was deceased.

If you were addicted to any substance or activity, you realized that that had happened when you were afraid to go to the next stage of life.

One or more of the six basic fears interfered with your growth: the fear of poverty, criticism, loss of love, illness, old age, or death. You are glad you had the courage to face and move through the challenges of that stage of life.

As you wrote about your children and grandchildren, you observed who played (and still plays) the roles in the Drama Triangle. Even in these situations, you won't let sentiment and family loyalty cloud your judgment. Instead, you do your best to be a good role model for them by walking your talk.

After you summarized your experiences with money, work, and love, you had a new appreciation for how hard it is to rewrite a life script so that it leads to a happy ending, a new appreciation for what you are up against personally and collectively. By *collectively*, I am referring to religious, historical, social, political, cultural, and family influences that pressure all of us to live life according to external standards. Once you stand up to these pressures, you don't judge yourself as harshly as you once did, nor do you judge others who are still under the spell of their life scripts or who have yet to find the strength to withstand external and internal pressure to conform.

You concluded your story by thanking (in an imagined dialogue) the supporting actors for their contributions to your life, beginning with your grandparents and parents. You are grateful for the gifts they gave you, no matter how small. Now that your expectations are realistic, you know they truly did the best they could, given their times, circumstances, and personal limitations.

Next you expressed your gratitude to your spouses and lovers for what you learned from them. Then you thanked the teachers and coaches who brought out the best in you. When it was appropriate, you wrote or called to express your thanks.

You also thanked (again, in an imagined dialogue) the people who taught you painful lessons. Had you understood what was going on back then, you would have walked down a different street. And now you do.

Step Four

The fourth step into the unknown was recognizing the passion clues that let you know you were on track and the signals that warned you when you were off, way off, track. Two of the passion clues that left a lasting impression on you were "you would do the work even if you did not get paid for it" and "you are focused on the process, not the outcome."

The two off-track signals you keep in mind when life feels out of control are "you worry about what others think" and "you take on more than you can handle." Moderation is not the most glamorous way to live, but you know now that it's the key to balance.

Step Five

You took the fifth step into the unknown when you identified your strengths, values, and needs. You were surprised to discover that your *strengths* were what you did easily and well. In fact, you thought everyone could do what you do naturally. Now you have a greater appreciation for your strengths, and so do the people you serve.

Your *values* were obvious once you watched what you did consistently. When confronted with life's problems, you like to tackle them head on (independence). If you need help, you enjoy talking things over with like-minded people (affiliation). When things are not working, you hold still until your intuition gives you a new way to look at the problem (creativity).

Your *needs* turned out to be the opposite of what the false self craved, since cravings are based on vanity. Your authentic self needs less, not more, of what burdens your spirit: possessions and superficial relationships. Solitude or a mixture of time with others and time alone turned out to be what sparked your creativity.

Maslow's hierarchy of needs showed you where you are on the pyramid that peaks with self-actualization, the desire to be the best you can be. Although you strive for excellence, you've learned to be content with where you are.

To help you identify your perfect niche in work, you wrote a list of your five strengths, five values, five needs, and temperament on a three-by-five card. On the back of the card, you wrote the five passion clues and five off-track signals.

You refer to your template for success when you need to make an important decision — such as whether to sign a contract, make an investment, or accept or reject invitations and offers of friendship — and when you must decide who gets your time and attention.

Step Six

The sixth step into the unknown was setting small goals that got you in the habit of succeeding. You learned that realistic goals have to match three criteria: measurement, motivation, and responsibility.

To make sure your goals were attainable, you wrote them down and gave them a six-month time frame, rewriting them until your subconscious accepted what you wrote as logical.

To visualize your goals, you made a collage of images and words you clipped from magazines or downloaded from Internet sites. Now when you read your written list and look at your collage, you feel connected to your authentic self.

Step Seven

With internal and external clutter out of your life, the next step was to learn how to recognize the passion clues and off-track signals. Then you identified your strengths, what you do easily and well. And then you identified your values, what you think is good, true, and worthwhile. Finally you made a list of your needs, what you must have to feel fulfilled. Then you were able to set small goals that led to the achievement of even greater goals.

The seventh step into the unknown was finding your perfect niche in work, the place where you could reach your full potential and make the money you need.

First, you narrowed the world of work down to five categories of interest, based on selections from the index section of your local "Yellow Pages" or from categories that you researched online. You read everything you could to prepare for meetings with people in these areas of interest.

If you were like Joanna when she was in her sixties, you didn't need to meet with anyone; all you had to do was streamline your surroundings so that you could focus on what you love. In her case, Joanna sold her parking-lot-sweeping business so she could concentrate on her pillow-cleaning business. Today Joanna's life is "an organized dream."

Or perhaps, like Mike, after you tried several options, you went back to your first loves, writing a book about sales and mentoring those who could benefit from your expertise. Or like Ann, you may have worked with another entrepreneur until you learned the basics of a business. Once you had enough experience, you went on your own, shaping the business until it matched your values and needs.

Perhaps you followed Kim's example. You contracted to provide your services to a business owner who needed your strengths to lighten her workload. Now you work at your own pace from your home office, relieved to have put nine-to-five workdays and long commutes behind you.

Or, after enough soul searching, you realized you were an introverted solo type who worked best alone, like Julie. You and your spouse reduced your debt so that you could begin the process of creating the niche where you could exceed your own and others' expectations. Once you were in your niche, you made sure that you continued to take small steps.

Whatever you decided to do, your perfect niche looks just like the images in your collage.

Step Eight

The eighth step into the unknown is not a step as much as it is a chance to put down your backpack and savor the view from the top: success on your terms. As you look back on the journey, you are amazed by the determination it took to create your happy ending.

The Happy Ending

A happy ending is not what you expected, is it? You thought that when you reached midlife and beyond, you would be too old, too ill, or too worn out to do what you always wanted to do. Or that you would be filled with regret and bitterness for what might have been had you only... (fill in the blank).

You expected money to be a constant worry because you would be living on a fixed or dwindling income, forgoing extras that add pleasure to life. Or you thought you might even be out on the street, homeless, poor, and with no one to care for you.

Or you expected that, if you were fortunate enough to have money, health, and loved ones, you would travel, take up hobbies, or buy nice things for people. Companions would be other retirees whose heyday was in the past, not the present. Your goal was to relax, play golf, and just hang out during the years before you died. For some people, this scenario is their happy ending, a time to kick back from a pressure-filled life. But for a creative person like you, this is just not enough. You have to be learning, growing, and contributing to your world or you go crazy, or you drive everybody around you crazy. The last thing you want is to wind up like people who die too early because they feel bored and useless.

By contrast, your life is an adventure that gets more exciting as you age, not the jump-up-and-down kind of excitement, but the quiet hum that comes from having a happy spirit. Since you are always changing and growing, you connect with all ages. In fact, you feel more relevant now than you did when you were in your twenties.

Now that you understand the past, you don't have to talk about it anymore. You are in the moment, acting on instinct at the right time and in the right place. It's safe to say that you're in tune with life's rhythms.

You are not afraid to look at the dark side of human nature, because you are well acquainted with your own darkness. You know the effort it takes to accept and integrate the shadow, personally and collectively. And you won't carry that burden for anyone, no matter how much you love them.

You used to push for what you thought you had to have, with the consequences ranging from mild to severe pain. But pain taught you self-restraint, to wait when all the signs said *wait*, and to view delays and setbacks as opportunities to review and reflect. The mistakes you made in the past were the best you could do at the time, given your level of awareness. And without those mistakes, you would not be the person you are today. You know when to say no, when to say yes, and when to say nothing.

Now it's time to savor success on your terms.

Success on Your Terms

Success means you do what you love and you make the money you need. This was not the definition of success Ann (discussed in the first chapter) had been taught from an early age. She thought success was when everybody was happy. Trying to reach this impossible goal kept her in a constant state of anxiety and frustration, until she let others be responsible for their happiness. Toward the end of our work together, I asked Ann to write about the person she used to be and how that differs from who she is today. "Email both descriptions to me when you're done," I said.

Ann's two summaries were such a fitting climax to our work together that I knew others would benefit from seeing them. With her permission I include what she wrote, edited for brevity and clarity.

After you read her descriptions, try the exercise yourself. You may find it as liberating as it was for Ann. First is her description of the person she used to be. Ann was surprised by how well she knew this person.

THE OLD ME

Ah...this is fun because I get to speak about who I used to be. Today this person turns me off completely, but I understand how she got that way. She is very controlling because she thinks she has to be "perfect," so perfect in fact that I want to run in the opposite direction from her.

For the old me, success means being a woman who is always rushing around to get things done. She never stops to think about what she needs, because she is too busy taking care of everybody else's needs. She holds back what she thinks and feels, because she is afraid others will get angry with her, and then she wonders why she feels isolated and alone. She is a slave to appearances, so she spends too much money on clothes, hairstyles, makeup, and the car she drives. Flatterers can fool her, because she craves admiration and attention.

My old self appears to be a hard worker, but the truth is she lacks focus and self-discipline. Because she is so scattered, she never gets where she wants to go, and she is envious of those who do. She may look good on the outside, but on the inside she's exhausted and lonely. There is no way on earth I can, or even want to, compete with this woman. Just the thought of her makes me feel uncomfortable and sad. No wonder I couldn't be happy before; she and I were at complete odds.

Next, Ann writes about the self she has come to know and love. Notice how definite she is. This is how you are when you know and accept yourself exactly as you are.

THE REAL ME

I need to go slowly. I hate feeling rushed. I like to think things through. I am happiest in simple, uncluttered surroundings. I find absolutely no meaning or pleasure in owning more than I need.

I need to rest and get plenty of sleep. I used to think I was lazy if I took time to rest and think. To compensate for feelings of guilt, I did too much and then felt tired and cranky, or I got sick. But I am a woman, not a machine.

As for work, I do what I love and I make the money I need.

This has been a total shock for me, because I thought I couldn't do what I wanted until I struck it rich. Now I know rich is living in the moment.

As for people, I love people, and by that I mean I love individuals. They intrigue me, and I am thrilled when something I do or say helps others to improve. I dislike superficiality and people who speak without saying anything. I've learned in those instances to be quiet.

I have an inner world that is creative and intimate. I love the life of the spirit. I love communion with God through prayer, and I feel this connection very deeply; it feeds and satisfies me. I love growing spiritually, being quiet so I can hear or sense those intuitive "nudges" from God.

What a remarkable transformation from the frustrated woman whose story opened this book. Can you see how accepting herself exactly as she is helped Ann to conquer the six basic fears: the fear of poverty, criticism, loss of love, illness, old age, and death?

The fear of poverty left the battlefield when Ann stopped measuring success by the amount of money she makes.

The fear of loss of love went down in defeat too, since the love that fills Ann's heart comes from a never-ending source of approval and affection.

Self-discipline put the *fear of criticism* out of commission once and for all.

As for the *fear of illness*, it's not the ogre it used to be now that Ann listens to her body. To her amazement, aging has become an ally, not an enemy.

The fear of old age doesn't glare back at Ann when she looks in her mirror, now that she appreciates the beauty wisdom brings. The winter of her life will be different from previous seasons, but it will be full of exploration and learning.

Ann went through the process of death and rebirth so many times that *the fear of death* has been transformed into a ruthless friend who clears away the old to make way for the new. She doesn't know what is going to happen when she dies, and she doesn't need to know until she gets there. Ann would rather savor the rewards of success on her terms: peace, prosperity, forgiveness, integrity, faith, tolerance, humor, growth, generosity, and joy.

Peace

Well, what do you know; peace came in on tiptoe, a quiet surprise. Ann thought there would be bells and whistles blowing loudly and banners waving all over the place when she reached the happy ending.

The inner war is over, so Ann has put away her defensive armor, trusty sword, and elaborate battle plans. All she needs now is awareness to protect her from self-injury.

Prosperity

Ann learned the hard way that abundance is the result of doing without until she can afford it. Now that she is debt-free, she buys only what she needs, and she purchases items that last, so she doesn't have to replace them. Extra money is invested wisely to reap the benefits of compound interest. Ann always has enough money, because she has all the money she needs (needs, not craves).

Forgiveness

Bitterness and regret are not for Ann. She knows she gave her all and that's what counts. She forgives because she wants to be forgiven. A wiser judge will take care of wrongdoers, of that she is sure.

Ann cannot fully comprehend everything, but she knows someday she will, if not in this life then the next. The good, the bad, the ugly, and the beautiful will all fit into the grand scheme of things.

Integrity

When in murky water, Ann becomes a deep-sea diver, finding nuggets of wisdom in the darkness. She rises from those depths richer than ever.

When she is with people she trusts, Ann is playful and funny. When she is around untrustworthy people, she is not there, meaning she does not engage.

Faith

Now that Ann has shaken off the shackles of self-doubt, she no longer swings between the extremes of hope and despair, either wild optimism or bleak pessimism. Ann trusts that outcomes will be better than anything she could plan, so she focuses on the day she is in, not on tomorrow.

Tolerance

There are many paths to the truth, not just Ann's. What she does know for sure is that everyone everywhere wants what she wants: health, freedom, work they enjoy, and loving relationships.

Ann chooses her words carefully because she knows words can hurt people. She says that those who have to be right will have to learn that reality always wins in the end. She would rather not have all the answers, just better questions.

Humor

Laughter is the sure cure for whatever ails Ann. To maintain her optimistic outlook, she watches funny movies and reads books about people who solve problems. Ann's favorite times are when she shares a good laugh with her best friend, her husband.

Growth

Ann does what scares her because that's how she grows. But she doesn't act without sizing up the consequences.

When life takes an unexpected turn, Ann flows along with what is happening, rather than resisting the inevitable. But if someone crosses her boundaries, she does something about it, instead of complaining or feeling like a helpless Victim.

Generosity

Everything comes back in equal measure, so Ann gives without expecting a return, knowing she will be fully compensated. She's nobody's fool, and she's also the best friend anyone could have. The golden rule starts at home, so Ann treats herself with courtesy and respect.

Joy

Ann has walked through the valley of the shadow into the light. She fears no evil because goodness and mercy are her constant companions. Her thoughts, feelings, and actions are in alignment most of the time now, not at odds the way they used to be.

Now that her karma sheet is clean, Ann feels free to celebrate each day as a new beginning. She has become the balanced, secure individual she was destined to be, and she feels great joy.

SUMMARY

1. Review the past to consolidate gains.
2. Prepare for the challenges that go with reaching your full potential.
3. Savor the upsides of success on your terms.
4. Celebrate freedom from the script.
5. Pass on what you learned.

Acknowledgments

W*ork with Passion in Midlife and Beyond* turned out to be a case of "I don't write what I know, I write what I need to know," to quote the late Don Graves, columnist for the *Boston Globe*.

Georgia Hughes, editorial director at New World Library, got me started on this project. The end result surprised both of us. Carol Craig (Editinggallery.com) and Janice Hussein (Documentdriven.com) offered many insightful comments and suggestions. Working with the editorial and marketing team at New World Library — Kristen Cashman, Jonathan Wichmann, Munro Magruder, and Monique Muhlenkamp — as well as copyeditor Bonnie Hurd and publicist Jane Wesman (Wesmanpr.com) was an enjoyable learning experience from start to finish.

I am thankful for the clients who so generously allowed me to use their stories after altering them to protect their privacy, especially "Ann" and "Mike." Thanks also to the clients who sent links and articles as I wrote the book. It's a privilege to work with such thoughtful, open-minded people.

And it's an added bonus to be related to some of my biggest fans. Thank you, Patrick, Renée, Patrice, and Mark, for your support and enthusiasm.

Finally, I am grateful for the love that is both deeply personal and universal to us all, regardless of how we experience the presence of God.

Notes

Chapter 1. Ann Rewrites Her Life Story

1. Stephen Karpman, MD, "Fairy Tales and Script Drama Analysis," *Transactional Analysis Bulletin* 7, no. 26 (April 1968): 39–43.

Chapter 2. Streamline Your Life

1. Adam Voiland, "Why Do We Make Bad Choices When We Know Better?" *U.S. News and World Report*, December 7, 2007, http://health.usnews.com/articles/health/2007/12/07/want -to-break-a-bad-habit-try-this.html.
2. Mick LaSalle, "'Revolutionary Road' Year's Best," *San Francisco Chronicle*, January 1, 2009.
3. "Old. Smart. Productive," *Business Week*, June 27, 2005. Another survey that validates this article indicates that 83 percent of boomers plan to keep on working after retirement. This statistic was mentioned during a report on boomers seeking fantasy jobs. *NBC Nightly News*, October 18, 2006, James Hattori reporting.

4. Ibid.

5. Jonathan Peterson, "Many Forced to Retire Early," *Los Angeles Times*, May 15, 2006. According to a McKinsey & Company survey of 3,086 people, 4 out of 10 retirees left their jobs sooner than expected, either because of health problems or loss of job. Many were sure they'd work past retirement age to supplement retirement funds, but only 13 percent accomplished that goal. What is shocking about this article is the lack of awareness on the part of the interviewees. This makes it even more urgent for boomers to start now to find the work they love.

6. "Doing Well by Doing Good," *Wells Fargo Small Business Roundup*, July 2007.

7. Napoleon Hill, *Think and Grow Rich* (New York: Fawcett Books, 1960). Written during the Great Depression, this book is still valid decades later. The prose may be a bit purple for the modern eye, but Hill's concept epitomizes the American comeback spirit.

8. Karen Kingston, *Clearing Your Clutter with Feng Shui* (New York: Broadway Books, 1999). Kingston covers much more than getting rid of material things. She takes a holistic approach to the subject of clutter, connecting the dots between outer balance and a balanced mind.

9. John E. Sarno, *Healing Back Pain: The Mind-Body Connection* (New York: Warner Books, 1991). This groundbreaking physician says what he thinks in the face of criticism from peers. Nothing is more authoritative than the doctor who heals himself.

10. Discussed on William Uzgalis's website, Great Voyages: The History of Western Philosophy from 1492–1776, Oregonstate.edu/instruct/phl302/philosophers/descartes. Uzgalis is an academic who loves his work and writes about Descartes' history and theory.

11. Sarno, *Healing Back Pain*, p. 85.

Chapter 3. Rewrite Your Life Story

1. Claude Steiner, *Games Alcoholics Play* (New York: Ballantine, 1971). I am greatly indebted to this humorous psychotherapist for his explanation of the life script and the illogical conclusion, or series of conclusions, that starts the life on a downward spiral and keeps it there until we decide to let go of faulty assumptions. As he demonstrates, when you love your work, helping others to change scripts can be fun.

2. Ibid.

3. Eric Berne, *Games People Play* (New York: Grove Press, 1964).

4. Steiner, *Games Alcoholics Play*, p. 13.

5. Jonathan Shay, *Odysseus in America: Combat Trauma and the Trials of Homecoming* (New York: Scribner, 2003). As a psychiatrist with the Department of Veterans Affairs, Dr. Shay treated hundreds of veterans with post-traumatic stress syndrome. He prefers to call this syndrome war's inevitable psychological injury, so that veterans do not think something is wrong with them when they suffer from the aftermath of combat.

6. Patricia Evans, *The Verbally Abusive Relationship* (Holbrook, MA: Adams Media, 1996). Evans says that verbal abuse is any expression that diminishes the spirit, from silence to sarcasm to violent outbursts (the Persecutor role in the Drama Triangle). If you are being verbally or physically abused and you think you deserve mistreatment, this book will help to correct that illogical assumption.

7. Nathaniel Hawthorne, *The Scarlet Letter* (New York: Pocket Books, 1976). Hester is the scapegoat for a community of Persecutors until she creates a life apart from them. Not a happy ending in the romantic sense, but happy when your definition of success is to become an individual.

8. John Keats, *The Norton Anthology of English Literature*, vol. 1 (New York: Norton, 1968), p. 570.

9. Stephen Karpman, MD, "Fairy Tales and Script Drama Analysis," *Transactional Analysis Bulletin* 7, no. 26 (April 1968).

10. John Milton, *The Norton Anthology of English Literature*, vol. 1 (New York: Norton, 1968), pp. 1025–26.

11. From http://grief.com/the-five-stages-of-grief/. David Kessler's home page discusses the five stages of grief: denial, anger, bargaining, depression, and acceptance. Kessler's compassion and understanding will help you feel the pain of loss and work through it.

12. Marti Laney, *The Introvert Advantage* (New York: Workman Publishing, 2003). Laney is a therapist and an introvert who writes with empathy about the introvert's need for solitude and space.

13. John Holt, *How Children Fail*, rev. ed. (Cambridge, MA: Da Capo Press, 1995); Holt, *How Children Learn*, rev. ed. (New York: Perseus, 1995). The Da Capo Press summarizes Holt's work: "First published in the mid 1960s, *How Children Fail* began an education reform movement that continues today. In his 1982 edition, John Holt added new insights into how children investigate the world . . . His understanding of children, the clarity of his thought, and his deep affection for children have made both *How Children Fail* and its companion volume, *How Children Learn*, enduring classics." See www.perseusbooksgroup.com/perseus/book_detail.jsp?isbn=0201484021 (accessed October 24, 2009).

14. Holt, *How Children Fail*, pp. 271–72.

15. John Holt, "Plowboy Interview," *Mother Earth News*, July–August 1980, pp. 11–16.

16. Portia Nelson, *There's a Hole in My Sidewalk* (Hillsboro, OR: Beyond Words Publishing, 1993).

Chapter 4. Recognize the Passion Clues and Off-Track Signals

1. John Middleton Murry, *Keats* (New York: Farrar, Straus & Giroux, 1968), p. 198. This erudite critic pays respectful tribute to a wonderfully gifted young man.

2. Ibid., pp. 68, 232–33, 261.

3. Krishnamurti, *The First and Last Freedom* (New York: Harper &
    Row, 1975), pp. 82, 68. My copy of this paperback is so worn that
    whole sections have separated from the binding, but I refuse to
    buy a new copy because then I would have to redo all the
    underlining. Living as he says is simple, but it is not easy.

4. From *Detachment*, a one-page pamphlet produced by Al-Anon.
    This pamphlet is a reprint from the group's annual letter for
    professionals (Al-Anon Family Group Headquarters, *Al-Anon
    Speaks Out*, 1979) and is offered at Al-Anon meetings as well as
    at www.al-anonny.org/detach.htm.

5. *Webster's New Collegiate Dictionary*, sixth ed. (Springfield, MA:
    G. & C. Merriam, 1979), s.v. "envy."

Chapter 5. Create a Template for Success

1. Calvin S. Hall and Gardner Lindzey, *Theories of Personality* (New
    York: John Wiley, 1970), p. 88. In this chapter, Hall and Lindzey
    describe Carl Rogers's unconditional-regard approach with
    clients. Rogers said that acceptance by the therapist creates a safe
    environment where clients can accept themselves.

2. Ibid., pp. 99–100.

3. Richard Ellmann, *James Joyce*, rev. ed. (New York: Oxford
    University Press, 1983), p. 3.

4. Vernon Howard, *The Power of Your Supermind* (Marina Del Rey,
    CA: DeVorss, 1975). Howard's books sold millions during his
    lifetime, and they still sell. His concept of the quiet mind is not
    new, but the presentation is uniquely his.

5. Ibid., p. 32.

6. Ibid., p. 31.

7. Ibid., p. 126.

8. http://psychology.about.com/od/theoriesofpersonality/a/
    hierarchyneeds.htm. This link summarizes Maslow's hierarchy
    and also offers a thoughtful critique of his theory.

9. Abraham Maslow, *Motivation and Personality* (New York: HarperCollins, 1943).

10. Benjamin Hoff, *The Tao of Pooh* (New York: E. P. Dutton, 1982), pp. 4–6.

11. D. G. Zyfowsky, "15 Needs and Values," *Vocational Guidance Quarterly* 18 (1970): 182.

12. Quoted in Hall and Lindzey, *Theories of Personality*, p. 534.

Chapter 6. Take Small Steps

1. Bill Parcells, *The Tough Work of Turning Around a Team* (Boston: Harvard Business School, 2007).

Chapter 7. Find Your Perfect Niche

1. Michael Phillips, *The Seven Laws of Money* (Menlo Park, CA: World Wheel, 1974), p. 9.

2. Mark Helow and Jim Schleckser, "From Entrepreneur to Leader," *Wells Fargo Small Business Roundup*, May 2007.

3. Ibid.

4. Ibid.

5. Gordon B. T. Mermin, Richard W. Johnson, and Eric J. Toder, *Will Employers Want Aging Boomers?* (Washington, DC: Urban Institute, July 2008), p. 31.

6. Joyce Lain Kennedy, *Resumes for Dummies*, 5th ed. (Hoboken, NJ: Wiley, 2007).

Chapter 8. Savor Success on Your Terms

1. Mick LaSalle, "Ask Mick LaSalle," *San Francisco Chronicle*, August 3, 2008.

Recommended Resources

Books

Erickson, Erik. *Childhood and Society*. New York: Norton, 1980. Erickson is known for his eight stages of human development theory: trust (ages 0–2), autonomy (2–5), initiative (5–8), industry (8–14), identity (14–25), intimacy (18–35), generativity (21–65), and integration (45–end of life). The latter two stages overlap, and they are the themes in *Work with Passion in Midlife and Beyond*.

Irving, John. *The Hotel New Hampshire*. New York: Ballantine, 1995. Irving's quirkiest story about a wildly dysfunctional family that travels from New England to Vienna and back is told with his usual black humor and ruthless honesty. As Irving says, "The characters in my novels, from the very first one, are always on some quixotic effort of attempting to control something that is uncontrollable — some element of the world that is essentially random and out of control."

Miller, Sue. *Family Pictures*. New York: Harper & Row, 1990. As in her first remarkable novel, *The Good Mother*, Miller writes with insight and heart about the tensions of contemporary family relationships. This story about a large, conflicted Chicago family spans forty years and tells of a generational script the two rebels in the family struggle to change.

Perera, Sylvia Brinton. *The Scapegoat Complex*. Toronto: Inner City Books, 1986. A hard-hitting book by a Jungian analyst who says the shadow consists of attitudes, behavior, and emotions that do not conform to the ego ideals of the individual and groups, which is why it is rejected and then projected onto handy scapegoats. Those who identify with the scapegoat (the Victim) take on rejected shadow qualities, causing them to suffer from others' shame and guilt. Giving back unearned shame and guilt restores mental balance.

Schnarch, David. *Passionate Marriage, Love, Sex, and Intimacy in Emotionally Committed Relationships*. New York: Henry Holt, 1997. Schnarch says a passionate marriage is the result of two individuals who hold on to their identities in close relationships. Both parties step up to the plate and admit mistakes, and both are able to self-soothe when anxious. Commitment is a prerequisite for personal growth, a people-making enterprise, he says. Casual relationships don't stir up fears and insecurities, and so they don't provoke growth, because they are too easy to leave.

Stout, Martha. *The Sociopath Next Door*. New York: Broadway, 2006. Stout is a Harvard psychologist who says that one out of twenty-five people falls into the category of the conscienceless. Her book shows why it's so easy to get entangled in dysfunctional patterns with Persecutors: their charm, spontaneity, and intensity easily seduce the unwary. Most important, Stout offers strategies for avoiding the power plays, flattery, and other games that such people use to entrap us.

Winspear, Jacqueline. *Pardonable Lies*. New York: Henry Holt, 2005. This is the third in a series of novels about Maisie Dobbs, "a heroine to cherish," as one reviewer said of Winspear's inspiring detective-psychologist. The books are set in London shortly after

World War I, but Maisie is for all time. Don't try the Drama Triangle on her!

Wroblewski, David. *The Story of Edgar Sawtelle*. New York: Harper-Collins, 2008. The Drama Triangle is presented in its most tragic form in this stunning first novel. Wroblewski's Hamlet-like young protagonist solves the mystery of his father's murder, and in the process he comes to terms with a mother who turns a blind eye to evil (the boy's Persecutor uncle). As you read, you will find yourself urging the hero to make different choices.

Websites

Aarp.org is the premier site for older Americans. You'll find helpful information about money, work, travel, and politics. You can also listen to AARP's radio host interviewing guests on various topics.

Cranky.com is an upbeat resource for boomers. Whether you want tips on buying a second home in Mexico, financial management, or relationships, the information you need is here.

Encore.org is based on Marc Freedman's book *Encore: Work That Matters in the Second Half of Life*. The information and links on this site will be useful after you've finished the internal work in *Work with Passion in Midlife and Beyond*.

Gapingvoid.com is Hugh MacLeod's irreverent site. You will feel encouraged and inspired by his popular download *How to Be Creative*. Hugh's thinking is the opposite of the Victim/Rescuer/Persecutor mentality.

Salary.com will help you determine the going rate for your strengths and experience in your geographic area.

Viastrengths.org is the website of Values in Action, an independent, nonprofit organization that supports the positive psychology approach. You can take their thirty-minute inventory to determine your strengths.

Television Shows

The Biggest Loser (www.nbc.com/The_Biggest_Loser/) shows why obesity is a self-destructive script. Two dedicated trainers use brutal honesty, praise, and common sense to encourage participants to give up roles in the Drama Triangle.

Chopped (www.foodnetwork.com/chopped/index.html). From the website: "Passion and expertise rule the kitchen on this fast-paced series. . . . The series challenges four up-and-coming chefs [many are in midlife and beyond] to turn a selection of everyday ingredients into an extraordinary three-course meal. After each course, a contestant gets 'chopped,' until the last man or woman left standing claims victory. Each week a rotating panel of culinary elite judges . . . decide whose dishes shine the brightest and award the winner $10,000."

Designed to Sell (www.hgtv.com/designed-to-sell/show/index.html) is a nightly program on HGTV that takes homeowners through the three stages of change. Designer Lisa LaPorta is just one of the talented stagers on this show who turn cluttered, outdated houses that won't sell into stylish, updated homes that do sell, all on a budget of two thousand dollars (and free labor from the show's carpenters).

Divine Design (www.hgtv.com/divine-design/show/index.html), another HGTV show, is also about the three stages of change. It features Candice Olson, Canada's leading interior designer. Check Candice's show schedules so you can see her remodel spaces with her masterful eye for detail and beauty.

Project Runway (www.mylifetime.com/on-tv/shows/project-runway), hosted by Heidi Klum and Tim Gunn, features designers who pit their skills against one another's for a big prize. On short notice and with a small budget, they must create garments that meet the high standards of celebrity designers and guests. Those who rise to the occasion go on to the next episode; those who don't go home.

What Not to Wear (http://tlc.discovery.com/fansites/whatnottowear
/whatnottowear.html) stars enthusiastic hosts Stacy London and
Clinton Kelly, who use humor and a no-nonsense approach to take
nominated guests through the three stages of change, from shock,
to resistance to change, to acceptance of a new and flattering appearance.

Index

About the Author

Nancy Anderson is an innovative career and life consultant and the author of the pioneering career guide *Work with Passion: How to Do What You Love for a Living* (New World Library, 1984; twentieth-anniversary edition, 2004).

Nancy was a Regents Scholar at the University of California, Riverside, where she graduated magna cum laude with an interdisciplinary degree in English and political science. Following graduation in 1976, Nancy started a career guidance firm in San Francisco with two partners. Five years later, in 1981, she started her own career consulting practice and wrote *Work with Passion*. Today, she still enjoys helping her clients find their perfect niche and writing about the process for publication. Nancy's website is www.workwithpassion.com.